Library Of
YEHUDA LEV
and
ROSEMARIE PEGUEROS-LEV

BEING AMÉRICA

ESSAYS ON ART, LITERATURE AND IDENTITY FROM LATIN AMERICA

Edited by Rachel Weiss
with Alan West

WHITE PINE PRESS

© 1991 Rachel Weiss

All rights reserved. This book, or parts thereof,
may not be reproduced in any form without permission.

Publication of this book was made possible, in part, by grants from
the National Endowment for the Arts
and the New York State Council on the Arts.

Cover photograph by Alfredo Jaar.

Book design by Elaine LaMattina.

ISBN 0-877727-02-4

WHITE PINE PRESS
76 Center Street
Fredonia, New York 14063

> "*1916: Columbus*
>
> *Latin America Invades the United States*
>
> Rain falls upward. Hen bites fox and hare shoots hunter. For the first and only time in history, Mexican soldiers invade the United States.
>
> With the tattered force remaining, five hundred men out of the many thousands he once had, Pancho Villa crosses the border and, crying "Viva México!", showers bullets on the city of Columbus, Texas."
>
> —Eduardo Galeano, *Memory of Fire: Century of the Wind*

Toward the new invasion, in which we all live.

CONTENTS

Preface - Alan West / 3
Introduction - Rachel Weiss / 7

MEMORY AND IDENTITY: SOME NOTES ON CULTURAL HISTORY

Memory and Identity: Some Historical-Cultural Notes
 - Elena Poniatowska / 13
Art and Identity in Latin America - Rita Eder / 28

NEW FORMS: CENTRAL AMERICA AND THE CARIBBEAN

Our Little Region - Claribel Alegría / 41
First Person Singular? - Norberto James / 51
Plastic Arts in Cuba - Gerardo Mosquera / 61

THE ENIGMA OF CHILE

Transcript of Remarks - Cecilia Vicuña / 73
Untitled - Marjorie Agosín / 77

Contents

CULTURE AND INDEPENDENCE IN PUERTO RICO
Culture and Independence in Puerto Rico - Martín Espada / 87
Untitled - Juan Sánchez / 96
Bregando - Luis Rafael Sánchez / 99

VISION, MYTH AND POWER
Poetics and Politics in Latin America - Julio Ortega / 109
Myth, Language and Politics - Alan West / 116
Transcript of Remarks - Alfredo Jaar / 123

NATIONALISM AND LATIN AMERICANISM
Identity as Women? The Dilemma of
   Latin American Feminism - Marta Lamas / 129
Does Art from Latin America Need a Passport?
   - Luis Felipe Noe / 142
Painting, Identity and the Pursuit of Happiness
   - Wilfredo Chiesa / 152
Questions from the audience / 156

SIGNS OF EVERYDAY LIFE
Transcript of Remarks - Carlos Capelán / 163
Transcript of Remarks - Cristina Pacheco / 170
Signs of Everyday Life - Francisco Méndez-Díez / 181

LATIN AMERICA IN NORTH AMERICA
Transcript of Remarks - Gerardo Mosquera / 189
Border Brujo - Guillermo Gómez-Peña / 194

Biographical Notes / 237

End Notes / 245

BEING AMÉRICA

PREFACE
BEING AMÉRICA OR
WHAT'S IN AN ACCENT

ALAN WEST

We are the dreams of Bolivár and Ché, haunted by the call for unity, for a giant homeland, for an immense collective effort of creation. And yet we are enmeshed in border wars, civil strife, revolutions, rigged elections and petty nationalisms.

We are an archipelago of cultures, languages, visions and identities that are vibrant, resistant and forceful. But we often don't speak to each other and instead speak through the mouths of elites who, more often than not, have their thoughts (and bank accounts) leaning toward Paris or New York.

We are a mirror that flickers with images of audacity, hope and imagination. Think of Tamayo, Frida Kahlo, Torres García or Mandive or in the social realm of Sandino, Martí, Zapata or Mariátegui. But that same surface hurls back ignorance, misery, exploitation and dictators.

We are mapmakers because América is still being shaped, created, invented. This is true because we are still building our

Preface

homelands or trying to liberate them. But we are also mapmakers because borders are becoming more fictitious or because we leave or are exiled and have to create new countries and realities where we wind up. As Guillermo Gómez-Peña has said: "Our generation belongs to the world's biggest floating population: the weary travelers, the dislocated, those of us who left because we didn't fit anymore, those of us who still haven't arrived because we don't know where to arrive at, or because we can't go back anymore."

We are storytellers because words are one of our last refuges. We tell jokes because reality is almost unbearable, we tell stories to console, entertain and to tell the truth. We use words to struggle, as an emblem of freedom, as a means of safekeeping our memory, of recapturing our history, as a way of maintaining a sense of community in the face of being uprooted. But we are weary of words, too, because they have been used to numb us, to sell us (and to sell to us), and to tell so many lies that silence has often become a badge of dignity.

"We are the dogmas of blood and soil", as Luis Cardoza y Aragón once said.

Being América.

With an accent.

Or with many accents: Spanish, Portuguese, English, French, Creole, Papiamento, Quiché, Mam, Cherokee, Quechua, Mapuche, Cree and Ojibwa, to name only a few.

Language defines our physical, psychological, ethnic/national and social identity. Words or their avoidance or their banishment can be powerful instruments of inclusion or exclusion. The word helicopter, for example, means little to most North Americans but to a Salvadoran or a Vietnamese it can mean terror, isolation, deprivation or death. To those living north of the Río Grande (yes, that needs an accent also) IMF is just another acronym for some obscure international institution: for Brazilians, Venezuelans or Dominicans it means tripling of bread prices, the inability to take even public transportation, the impossibility of buying a book since it has become a luxury. In short, IMF means hunger.

There is a visual language as well that shapes the way we produce, look at, and receive images. It is the light of the Caribbean, or the way we draw our maps or the way we reconstruct our daily lives, like Juan Sánchez does with his "rican-structions", made out of flags, photos, newspaper clippings, drawings, inscriptions and religious icons. Or the way Alfredo Jaar questions our perception of "otherness" (probably one of the most detestable and imprecise words to be used in recent years), of misery, of exploitation and our complicity with its continuance.

Luis Felipe Noé wonders about the value of attributing national characteristics to works of art and whether or not Latin American art needs a passport at all. We all know too well that passports are devised to keep people from crossing borders, which is why we view them with suspicion. And perhaps it is difficult for some to understand why we get upset that Salvadorans might earn $150 for an eighty-hour work week and then be berated for not speaking English. It is these attitudes that find nothing wrong in sending millions to military governments in Latin America that murder, incarcerate and disappear their citizens, invade our countries under the flimsiest of pretexts, and punish countries that actually try to implement land reform, feed their people and give them adequate health care.

These are the apostles of purity and they exist not only in North America but in our native countries as well. Clinging dearly to the concept of a monocultural, monoreligious and monolingual society, purists impose homogenous schemes on their peoples, be it with TV sets or bayonets. They ignore, as Salman Rushdie pointed out, that the migrant condition "can be derived as a metaphor for all humanity". Indeed, we stumble on cities where there's snow but we dream with a sliver of beach and sun light. In our veins we bring with us one country and in our wanderings we build an imaginary one that maybe our children will inhabit.

We are drifters: there are Argentineans in Mexico and Spain, Chileans in Venezuela and Sweden, Cubans in Puerto Rico, Salvadorans in Nicaragua, Uruguayans in Cuba and lots of us from all our countries in the U.S. We are interminglers, clashing, assimilating and remaking our own and other cultures. We are beginning to "celebrate hybridity, impurity, and intermingling . . .we rejoice in mongrelization and fear the absolutism of the Pure". (Rushdie) Not all of us do but it is important to note that the first steps are being taken and they are a refreshing antidote to narrowness and ignorance.

Preface

These first steps come from a sense of loss (of culture, family, language, country), but at the same time a wider expressiveness, a plurality of vision, and a grater tolerance are to be gained.
Being América.
We improvise our own documents.
We spill across borders, defiant, hopeful and desperate.
We split up, accumulate, patch visions and realities together blissfully ignorant of labels.
We ridicule, spit at dogmas, retrench and go forward.
We make our own light by wandering.

INTRODUCTION

The papers and dialogues collected in this book are the result of a festival held in the Fall of 1988 at the Massachusetts College of Art titled "Latinoamérica Despierta: Art, Literature and Identity in Latin America Today." The generative idea of the festival was simple: to bring together a wide array of artists and writers, from all over Latin America, to present and discuss their work within the context of the social struggles and changes which are ubiquitous in the region. The festival goal was equally straightforward: to present, to a North American audience, an unmediated, first-hand encounter with diverse aspects of Latin American culture, in order to foment a process of dialogue and understanding. Much of our motivation came from the increasing Latinization of the U.S., the growing impact of Latin America and Latin Americans on life and policy in the U.S., and, the nearly impenetrable dis- and mis-information which stands in for fact regarding the region.

The efforts of many extraordinary people contributed to whatever success we have had in this project. First among these, of course, are the contributors, who traveled to Boston, often in the midst of too many other commitments, to participate in the dia-

Introduction

logues that we were attempting to build. They were, without exception, generous with both time and attention, and they all have my sincere thanks for making themselves so readily available.

The Massachusetts College of Art, under the auspices of its Visiting Artists Program, made contributions to this project too numerous to list here. The Massachusetts Council on the Arts and Humanities, through its Art Exchange Program, provided early and substantial funding for the festival. The Council's genuine commitment to cultural self-determination for all peoples, which it has pursued despite increasingly aggressive challenges, has helped create an atmosphere in the Commonwealth which makes possible projects such as this one. Also in this regard, the Massachusetts Foundation for the Humanities and Public Policy reacted enthusiastically, and generously, to our plans and notions.

Additional support for the festival was provided by grants from the Bank of Boston, the New England Foundation for the Arts, the Houghton Mifflin Company, New England Telephone and the National Endowment for the Arts. Roxbury Community College and especially Professor Tom Reeves and Dean Henry Allen provided facilities, energy and invaluable insight. Casa Latina in Northampton made possible extension programs which added enormously to the reach of the project. The Boston *Phoenix* and WBZ-TV's *Centro* made certain that word of the programs got out.

One primary commitment, made at the early stages of planning the festival, was that all participants should be invited to speak in the language of their choice. Especially in the midst of virulent "English-only" battles being waged against Spanish-speakers and other linguistic minorities in Massachusetts and elsewhere in the country, we were determined to provide a genuinely open forum in which the vehicle of address would not be cut off from the content through jingoistic assimilationist arguments. Helpful in formulating this, and then essential in carrying it out was Camilo Pérez-Bustillo.

The transition from festival to book was an arduous one, and I am grateful to Cola Franzen, who worked long hours out of sheer enthusiasm and friendship to transform a group of disparate papers into a continuous text which preserves the voice of the speakers and the sense of their presentation. Alan West, whose participation in this project ranged from the least to the most demanding aspects, has been much more than invaluable as advisor, contributor, conspirator, ally and friend.

Finally, although I generally mistrust panegyrics, I need it to acknowledge the extent of the contributions made by Luis Camnitzer. The continual stream of ideas, opinions, advice and information that he provided made this project first a possibility and later a reality. As a friend and as a colleague he has been unique and irreplaceable, and I thank him.

Two people invited to participate in the programs in Boston were refused permission to enter the United States. They are Ernesto Cardenal, poet and then Minister of Culture of Nicaragua and Pedro Alcántara, painter and Senator for the Unión Patriótica in Colombia. Both were excluded as a result of policies and practices which place political partisanship above free speech and other Constitutionally-guaranteed rights. In the spirit of open exchange, and out of respect for their extraordinary work as artist-statesmen, this book is dedicated to them.

Rachel Weiss
Neshkoro, Wisconsin, August 1989

MEMORY AND IDENTITY:
SOME NOTES ON CULTURAL HISTORY

MEMORY AND IDENTITY: SOME HISTORICAL-CULTURAL NOTES

ELENA PONIATOWSKA

What signs identify a person? Personal traits, sex, age, the color of the eyes, height, one or another scar, eyeglasses, a mole above the mouth. That is, if they should happen to have a passport or an identity card, a license to exist on Earth, permission to just be, an academic transcript. In Latin America, how many have credentials? Of course the poor and many of the *campesinos* who clamored with Zapata for "Bread and Freedom" don't. They go through life venerating their well-kept documents like an effigy of the Virgin of Guadalupe, taken back and forth to México City in their knapsacks, the yellowing deed that grants them the sacred ownership of their land, a legacy of their parents, handed over to them by the blessed revolution and which the Agrarian Reform Ministry does not accept as proof of land ownership, because in México land is dealt out in layers until you arrive at the very center of Hell.

What signs identify a country? The space it takes up on Earth, its years in existence, starting from the moment it was discovered and baptized (Latin America is barely a lion's cub; it will be 500 years old in 1992); its development, that is, its trajectory in the history of the universe; its personal history of conquest, invasion, violence, repression, the loss of its political sovereignty, its gradual emancipation, its idiosyncracies (a word I dislike). I prefer speaking of a country's character, its particular way of being which subsists despite colonial terrorism's legacy which destroyed its idols and altars; the massacre which, nonetheless, did not wipe out its spirit—so that Tonatzín is still our little mother nested in the Virgin Mary brought from Spain; or, to speak of its inner force or its sublime indifference, which enable it to live on the edge of tragedy.

If it were possible to observe from a spaceship the evolution and revolutions that have taken place on the continent called America, starting from when Christopher Columbus stumbled on it in 1492 as he sought other lands, we would see how unexpected and, therefore, how different the countries are from each other, and we'd come to the conclusion that the only thing that truly unites us is language, exploitation and poverty. To call this a "discovery," of what not only was already discovered but also inhabited and blessed with a culture that antedated the Christian era, is simply European arrogance. For the redskin, the Aztec, the *purepecha*[1], the Inca, the *gigantón* from the Patagonian region, it was an encounter with unknown inventions like gunpowder and the wheel; with the horse, that would turn the conquistadors into centaurs; with a different system of writing; and, with ambitions so grandiose and unheard of, with a different God though similar to the one imagined (Quetzalcoatl); and with a lost war.

The cosmographers of the period (Europeans, naturally) started with a few initial facts in tracing the maps of the continent, which they divided into fragments, showing islands where there was land, putting a continent where the islands were located, depicting an ocean instead of a river and thereby misleading the navigator by guiding him into blind alleys under the idea that they were straits; all of this in a gigantic and blundering jigsaw puzzle. And it seems that this cartography of lands blown out of the heavens, obsessed by mermaids and snails, cute little up-turned waves and crisscrossing rivers, mountains stretched out in the sun like rope put out to dry, borders cross-stitched and about to unravel, groves and corn patches which climb up in all directions, have perpetuated the confusion of this initial mapmaking; and so, the boundaries of the countries sway in the breeze and the rivers poke around where they don't belong and the waterfalls of Iguazu fall in Portuguese and its nationalistic roar no longer makes sense since the awe-struck eyes that see it know that it belongs to all humanity.

Isolated and weak, we're still suffering from this ignorant blundering or mistreatment by the mapmakers. Now it is the U.S. which sketchily outlines us and sinks us beneath the exhausting, immense weight of debt, because the greatest yoke in Latin America is its foreign debt.

In Latin America today, we know more about each other than what the colonizers knew back then. There is no real difference between México and Perú, no real difference between a Bolivian and a Mexican miner, a Nicaraguan and Salvadoran peasant, or one from Guatemala or Honduras; a woman from Pachuca (México) who sells corn meal pies is the same as a woman who sells *salteñas* in La Paz (Bolivia), and our slit-eyed children are extraordinarily alike. Rigoberta Menchú is the same as a *Mazahua* Indian (of México) who perches on a clump of earth selling gum, only she stands tall because of her self-respect and the strength of the Guatemalan struggle. It's the same with Domitila, the wife of the Bolivian miner, who asked permission to speak to the world. Domitila transcends her circumstances but she's like any robust and determined trinket-maker from Tlanepantla (México). The *Chamula* Indian Juan Pérez Jolote could've been born in Guatemala as well as in his native Chiapas, and the Salvadoran soldiers are just like our khaki-outfitted and dark-skinned Juans. We're very close to each other but we don't know it. It's true, before we were more like each other, our likeness was very intense and continues to be, but to avoid becoming aware of it, the illusion of national cultures, idiomatic expressions, typical dresswear, regional dishes and cultural impositions butt in.

That saying, of going from the frying pan into the fire ("salir de Guatemala para ir a Guatapeor"), proves that we're still not proud of being Latin Americans. Poor relatives don't get the same treatment as rich ones, and our Latin American identity has a lot to do with our behavior since we always live waiting for the catastrophe which will annihilate us.

Ours is a history of misery and abandonment and no philoso-

Memory and Identity

pher has truly defined us, no philosopher has taught us to be proud of ourselves. The presidents of all our countries are accustomed to yielding to the U.S., and their most important relationship is with North America. Among themselves they treat each other with familiarity, but up against the U.S. they're extremely cautious because they are always on the defensive. Roque Dalton, the poet, was right when he wrote:

> At the moment the President of my country
> happens to be Colonel Fidel Sánchez Hernández.
> But General Somoza, the President of Nicaragua,
> is also the President of my country.
> And General Stroessner, the President of Paraguay,
> is also a little bit the President of my country,
> although less so than the President of Honduras
> . . .
> And the President of the United States is more
> the President of my country
> than the President of my country.

Nowadays we go a long time without having news of each other. Yes, we eventually find out but without a sense of continuity and, above all, we stay in touch thanks to our common plight as debtors. Bolívar's dream continues to be just that, one sweet dream. In 1910 José Enrique Rodó[2] wrote: "I always believed that in Our America it wasn't possible to speak of many homelands, but of a great, unique homeland." If Rodó were to return, he'd be surprised to see how this indispensable unity has been postponed in favor of a systematic cultivation of non-communication. We're so near each other but don't know it. For Hispanic Americans, the homeland is Spanish America, added Rodó, and during his life he propagated the idea of a Spanish America conceived as a great and imperishable unity, a sublime and great homeland with its heroes, its educators, its tribunals: from the Gulf of México to the everlasting ice of the South. He placed the construction of this great homeland in the hands of writers: "Neither Sarmiento[3] nor Bilbao[4], nor Martí[5], nor Bello[6] nor Montalvo[7] are writers of one or another part of America, but instead of an American (continental) intellectuality."

Elena Poniatowska

The Latin Americanists, José Carlos Mariátegui[8] (Perú), José Enrique Rodó (Uruguay), José Martí (Cuba), José Vasconcelos[9] (México), José María Morelos[10] (México)—how many Josés!, all Josés, and where's the Virgin and above all the baby Jesus, boy or girl, whose paternity they aspired to and so they could be called America-Unified-Homeland?—were the makers of this homeland to which we belong in different ways, but with an intensity equalled by the expressions of oppression and repression, by the certitude of language, by our common enemies. If those who unified our continent in one sole aspiration were to return today, they would find us in the same fix; the size of the country matters little, or whether we are a continent. Each one of us is alone, and discord is renewed by those few in charge who claim to represent the national good. Neither El Salvador nor Honduras hate Nicaragua, but the news media and the confusion generated by the ruling classes give the appearance of national disputes. If we follow the map further south we see the conflicts between El Salvador and Nicaragua flare up, the creation of Panamá, sliced, or better yet, mutilated by the Canal; we see Bolivia and its historical insistence on gaining an outlet to the sea through the Atacama Desert, and Argentina at war with Paraguay in the Chaco border region[11]. From the border wars to the "Soccer War," all of it seems like a continuous effort to obtain more definite and definitive separations.

Spain's initial division of Latin America into viceroyalties shortly after the *Cortes* of Cádiz, during colonial times, found itself confronted by the mid-19th century with the newly-formed republics in open disputes over territories with unclear borders, much as in the current unresolved case (despite international arbitration) between México and the United Kingdom. What we call Belize is for the U.K. British Honduras, and Guatemala also claims the territory for its own, along with an undefined zone along the Suchiate River. During various decades, the area of Soconusco and the Mexican annexation of Chiapas was a matter of international controversy. The same kind of litigation goes on, but they are not conflicts between peoples, but of the elite. Argentina looks at treacherous Albion and at the witch of the Falklands, Mrs. Thatcher, and México, which in the time of President Echevarría aspired to be a great leader of the continent, has to settle for

Memory and Identity

recovering the lost half of its territory through migration. How many Mexicans there are in the U.S.! How many Latin Americans come up from the south looking for work that their countries can't offer them, in large part because the U.S., the richest and most advanced country in the world, rigs the rules of the game.

Bernardo Quintana, Mexican builder and engineer, founder of the best construction firm in Latin America and winner of many prizes for large scale projects, used to say that for him it was difficult to build in Central America because a dam that began in Honduras would end up in El Salvador. Like someone playing musical chairs where half a rump ends up on someone else's chair, the contracts had to be signed with both countries since the project would be straddling both. Quintana coined a phrase as much disparaging as illustrative of a point: "Why don't all these little countries join together?"

In fact, over the five hundred years of our existence, history shows that our cultural communication has been more with Europe, with those very same people who colonized us and crushed our customs, thereby giving us their own culture, than with each other. Right now, in the twentieth century, we look more to the U.S. and its silver screen technological breakthroughs for this cultural link than to anyone else. As Jesusa Palancares says to her husband Pedro Aguilar in *Hasta no verte Jesús mío*[12]: "When you're going to cheat on me, go for something classy, a white broad who's worth it, not someone dark-skinned and Indian like me." We are the natural market of the U.S., we are its "banana republic," its American Smelting, its Ocean Pacific, its United Fruit, we are its non-replenishing natural resource, we are its ill-paid workers, we are its cheap labor, its "brownies" and its "little Mexican jumping beans," we are its little monkeys, its banana-picking apes and the worst of it is between Blacks and Indians, for we don't acknowledge ourselves. We speak the same language, that's true, we more or less have the same handicrafts because all the impoverished countries share a common denominator which is popular art, a product of ingenuity and generosity, but the differences, the litigation about border areas, continues as the rule of the day and the "Latin American ideal" is confronted, as it was at the turn of the century, with a nationalism manipulated by local oligarchies. Our cultural nourishment is sought beyond our borders, but not in Venezuela, not in Perú, not in Guatemala, but in North American universities and their active Spanish and Portuguese departments (Julio Cortázar used to say that by teaching two months in the U.S. he could live in Paris for a year without working). And still the definitive sanctification comes to us from the U.S. and Europe, not from Brazil or Argentina. Still, all in all, Latin American unity has not been shattered, since the people of all our countries have an astonishing capacity to resist.

Spain was able to obtain a majority of the territory, but never a sense of unity. That's because the primitive colonies of England (which became the U.S.), Portugal, Holland and France maintained, at one point or another in history and up to the present, their sovereignty over islands and territories from the Southern Cone (the Malvinas) to the North Atlantic (the Bermudas), passing through the Guyanas, Belizes, Guadeloupes, Martiniques, Haitis, Puerto Ricos, Great and Smaller Caymans. Can we speak of a unity among the population? Of a geo-political unity? Yes, because despite everything, Latin American unity has not been shattered.

The conquistadors themselves found a continent inhabited by ethnic groups that were or were not related, groups with different as well as similar religions, diverse languages; they found a literature of the *Nahuatl*[13] and a philosophy of the *Maya* and *Quechua*[14], Mayan science and mathematics. It was the conquistadors who gave us our current Latin American identity by imposing their language, their idea of family, their Catholicism, their patriarchy, their *machismo* (I don't know anything about *machismo* in the indigenous population but, on the contrary, *Nahuatl* philosophy speaks of a feminism, at least of the care that a young woman must have for her body, of her body which is her honor, with expressions like my necklace of fine pearls, my *cuentita,* my little girl, my plume of quetzal, my daughter).

Nowadays, as the diversity of languages is being lost, we truly suffer a new loss; progressively our wealth diminishes, absorbed through assimilation or destroyed by the mass media. The *Chavo del 8*[15] and the *Chapulín Colorado*[16] have unified the language spoken by the children of Perú, Colombia, Guatemala and México. Whatever localisms and slang have wrought asunder, soap operas have brought together. Nonetheless there is a profound idiomatic

Memory and Identity

resistance that the mass media will never be able to destroy. Cervantes will always be more important than Raúl Velasco, and the ancient voice of *Araucaria*[17] will always come out on top. Reading and writing are the basis of our cultural resistance and the archaic languages of the people form part of their soul. It is something like its spirit. A novel like *Pedro Páramo,* written in Mexican, rings truer than all the soap operas by Lucía Méndez or Verónica Castro. We are offering a series of idiomatic pleasures which are important. Rulfo in Mexican, Cabrera Infante in Cuban and Cortázar with his short stories and hopscotches in River Plate parlance. *Boquitas pintadas,* by Manuel Puig, speaks the language of the Argentinian middle class, understood in all of Latin America. *La guaracha del macho Camacho (Macho Camacho's Beat)* by Luis Rafael Sánchez, written in Puerto Rican, has enthusiastic readers all over Latin America. At the same time the Spanish or Castilian we speak in America needs a dictionary more and more, since it is evolving toward what in the future will be Mexican, Argentinian, Cuban, Chilean, Salvadoran. Because in Chile children are called *guaguitas* and in Cuba the same word means bus; and because in México *concha* is a crusty, white, round and sweet bread whereas in other countries it stands for the female sexual organ, and despite the fact that it very well might have these traits, it is subject to all kinds of license, poetic and otherwise.

The efforts to unify our countries—at least in terms of foreign policy—or give them a unified presence to the rest of the world, is a rosary made of failures. You only have to look at the OAS and the way it is stymied and undermined, according to whose hegemony is being favored or affected. The efforts made by Contadora, which México can be proud of, have not diminished North-South tension. However, even though Contadora can't convince U.S. imperialism of anything (because you can never convince any imperialism of anything), it has helped avoid bloodshed. America means all of us, those in the South and those in the North, and Guillermo Haro, an astronomer who knew how to look at the Earth from the sky, used to get very upset when the U.S. appropriated for itself the term "we Americans" when it refers only to North Americans and the rest, that is the majority, is made up of us latinos, the inhabitants of Central and South America.

With the exception of the immigration from the Orient to

America, there has been a marked reduction in the European immigration to our continent from what it was in the past. We are no longer a promised land, especially since World War II. It never crosses the European mind any more to "do the Americas," nor to set sail with an ill-shaped bundle of hard bread, cheese and a bottle of olive oil in the hold of a ship, only to be put in quarantine on Ellis Island or the Isle of Triscornia. Those times are long gone and, aside from the misery, in Latin America there are revolutions, uprisings and massacres. Now immigration goes from South to North because part of the continent, disunited, has nothing to offer its inhabitants; and the sun is over there and it's a green sun, worth more than any of the poor coins that pass from one hand to another. ALAC (The Latin American Association of Free Trade) had an ephemeral existence. The mercantile traffic of the windward armada or the voyages from México to the Philippines were, proportionately, more important and of greater commercial value, taking into account colonial census figures, than the current traffic between Latin American countries. Coffee, sugar, tin, copper, silver, gold, vanilla, hemp, oil and many other goods go from our countries to other regions, but with a price set by international consumers.

But Latin America doesn't let Rodó down as far as his phrase about the citizens of a (Latin) American intellectuality is concerned, because of the names of Sarmiento, Bilbao, Martí, Bello and Montalvo; you can add Gallegos, José Eustacio Rivera, Guiraldes, López Velarde, Vallejo, Neruda, Asturias, Carpentier, Borges, Paz, Fuentes, García Márquez, del Paso, Luis Cardoza y Aragón and many others. So many others I haven't named so as not to sound like a phone book, writers of such stature like Lezama Lima and Juan Carlos Onetti and others who conquered the word, the nationalisms, the dream of the Liberator, Bolívar's Ideal, a moral unity above all discrepancies and nationalisms within the continent. It is not in vain that Juan Rulfo was the Mexican who knew the most about Brazilian literature, and you'd have to hear him speak about Guimaraes Rosa, Mario de Andrade, Rubem Fonseca, Lygia Fangundes Telles and Jorge Amado. And it's not for naught that novels reflect the Latin American situation, at times one of terror, as in the case of Galeano, Sábato, Marta Traba, Luisa Valenzuela and Elvira Orphée, who know very well about persecution, jail and death.

The most vigorous possibility of unity among the countries, from the time of the *caudillos*[18] of the independences (yes, in plural) whose ideal took root and crystallized, fragile as crystal, failed. And like glass, it is a seduction made of images which failed with Bolívar himself. Those who followed were dictators, or paved the way for dictatorships in the continent. The independent countries of America never even agreed on the same type of rule of law, the same system of government or the same degree of independence; there are dictatorships, centralized republics, federal republics, and regimes that are more or less socialist. The majority of them adopted a federal system imitating North American federalism, where it was genuine—given that it resulted from a pact of federation among the first colonies, independent amongst themselves, with inhabitants of different backgrounds, religions, languages and customs. The centralism which ruled Hispanic America for four hundred years saw itself transformed by an act of grace and edicts into federal republics which only obeyed the center of power.

The most enticing thing, from a literary point of view, is the figure of the dictator—truly fabulous. Antonio López de Santa Ana, eleven times President of México between 1833 and 1855, ordered funeral rites and a burial for his left leg lost in battle. And so his funeral became history (we have to agree it's more original than Caligula naming his horse as consul). And of Alvaro Obregón, third Mexican President after the revolution, one cannot properly say he was a dictator. In the monument to Obregón next to my home in Chimalistac, which is yours as well, the invitation is open and standing, his left hand lost in combat is preserved. My small children asked me, not too long ago, as a reward for their good grades, that I take them to see Obregón's hand preserved in a huge mausoleum in a jar of alcohol. Perón had Evita embalmed, and more people have filed past her body than Stalin's, since she was prettier. Her body disappeared for twenty years, only to reappear in 1975. Luis Cardoza y Aragón remembers General Jorge Ubico, the dictator of Guatemala who was toppled in 1944. He would sit his generals in a specially-built dentist's office in the National Palace and yank their teeth out without using anesthesia, deriving pleasure from the screams of his uniformed gorillas. The very same Ubico would put on a record of classical music and since he had a drum set for playing jazz he would drum away to spoil Chopin, Bach or Vivaldi. You could fill page upon page about the peculiarities of Latin American dictators. You see, therefore, we almost have no need for novels since our surprising reality far outstrips the world of fiction. That's when we realize that our reality described as surreal is really in line with the order of the day. This is when the magical-realism of Alejo Carpentier began to take shape and the novels about dictators (one dictator for all of them, Juan Manuel de Rosas who is Porfirio Díaz, who is Vicente Gómez, who is Doctor Francia, who is Guzmán Blanco, who is Trujillo, who is Somoza—each one with his different eccentricities) which are *The Autumn of the Patriarch, El Recurso del Método, I, The Supreme,* and *The Death of Artemio Cruz.* All the great solitary figures of the Palace (who were at one time revolutionaries) together formed what could be called one sole novel of the dictator written with a totalizing will amongst Alejo Carpentier, García Márquez, Augusto Roa Bastos and Carlos Fuentes. These writers, in their visions, could well be weaving amongst themselves the great Latin American magic carpet, that cape draped over the shoulders of Bolívar's dream, a cloak that stretches from North to South. A gigantic text of the dictatorship which is biography, history and delirium, because nothing is as grotesque as those delirious tropical Latin American dictators who would ship Eiffel Towers, little Versailles, Schonbrunns and Puertas del Sol from Europe while the *guiros* and *maracas*—the most sensual instruments on Earth—are playing. America's history is like no other: magical and Faustian, black and white, miraculous and terrible, real and incredible; because for us, what is common fare is for Anglo Saxons nothing less than incomprehensible and absurd, despite the fact that in their childhood they read *Alice in Wonderland,* just as we cannot understand either, let's be clear, how a third-rate actor could twice be President of the United States.

Our perception of the world has little to do with Europe's or North America's (the latter composed, above all, of European emigrations), and it is only now that, culturally speaking, Chicanos are being taken into account, the ancient Mexicans and previous owners of the territory north of the Río Bravo[19]. All those "wet-

Memory and Identity

backs" of the continent who are muleteers and who take to the road, come to the United States to stay and don't return to their country of origin, the hispanics, the "wetbacks," the latinos, and it's only now that this phenomenon is being analyzed. Which begins to give us a proper definition of the latino being. But another phenomenon of Latin America is exile. Writers who have had to leave their countries because of dictatorship, like Onetti, Benedetti, Galeano, Cristina Peri Rossi, David Viñas have lived in Spain, as has the Chilean novelist José Donoso. Uruguay, a country of three million, lost six hundred thousand; there are seven hundred thousand Argentinians out of Buenos Aires. (México has taken in thousands of refugees; it was the first to open its doors to Chileans after Allende. Argentinians, Uruguayans, Salvadorans, Guatemalans—for years the poet and art critic Luis Cardoza y Aragón has lived among us, and he can't return to Guatemala because they would kill him like they killed Alaide Foppa.) To sum up, all this is shaping a profile of Latin American-ness, of those who have to leave their countries for political reasons, as many abandon home for what they call "need"—a need synonymous with hunger and also with political failure because in the last instance, they are political emigrés because their government has offered them nothing—no Agrarian Reform, nor jobs, nor civil rights.

What does Latin Americanness consist of? Obviously where it is most visible to the world is in the eyes of others, especially Europeans who differentiated us and to whose family we aspired to belong during the first half of this century. I refer, naturally, to literature; we have venturously become independent of Europe and nowadays our visibility is constructed with our own eyes, and with our own look we see our hunger, our misery, our repression, our militarism, our ideology and that new form of torture so uniquely Latin American, the "disappearance," which wipes us off the face of the Earth like it wiped away the Argentinian writers Harold Conti and Rodolfo Walsh.

From this totalizing impact brought forth by writers, be it in terms of magical-realism or of magical-frightfulism, comes the fact that great writers have been called upon to occupy public office. Juan Bosch and Rómulo Gallegos have been presidents of their countries. Ernesto Cardenal was Minister of Culture of Nicaragua.

Gabriel García Márquez has been proposed as a candidate for President of his country, and he has declined it wearing the same *guayabera* he wore to receive the Nobel Prize. On various occasions successive governments (of México) have offered Octavio Paz official positions, and his name as well as that of Carlos Fuentes is a front-runner for the Minister of Foreign Relations. This follows a long tradition of diplomat-writers throughout Latin American history with figures such as Alfonso Reyes, Pablo Neruda, Enrique González Martínez and Miguel Angel Asturias. Even today Mario Vargas Llosa wants to be President of the Republic of Perú and, if the Cardenista movement were to triumph, Carlos Monsiváis would surely be named Minister of the Interior or Chief of Police. One has to ask: Magical-realism or Magical-frightfulism?

It pleases me to agree with Rita Eder when she says that the period between 1920 and 1945 was a time when "the ideal of a Latin American culture gathered strength as a manifestation of political unification put forth by Martí and later Vasconcelos, Mariátegui and Haya de la Torre, among others."

Through the word, Latin America has become unified, from the Río Bravo to Tierra del Fuego. Through the word we safekeep our memory. The word has been an instrument of struggle, the word has made us laugh, and the word has risen up against silence and suffering. The dearest things I know about Latin America I know from its writers, filmmakers, photographers, painters, sculptors, musicians, choreographers and dancers. The most depressing things I've learned from its presidents and politicians.

To begin singing I first want to ask permission and beg forgiveness for these jottings which like the image of Latin America I toss out haphazardly, like the woman who casts her sorrows to the wind (at least that's what the song says). We are still not a solid block of thought, but I think we're headed toward a literature in Latin America in which it won't be Enrique Molina who narrates the life of Camila O'Gorman and her lover, the priest Ladislao Gutiérrez shot by firing squad on orders of the dictator Rosas, but instead the very nuns will tell their story, the very same Liberation Theology priests. It will no longer be José María Arguedas who brings the indigenous people into his narrative, but instead it will be the Indians themselves who speak without the

Memory and Identity

need of Ricardo Pozas and they will do it through the voice of Juan Pérez Jolote. It won't be Manuel Scorza who achieves their vengeance, but they themselves who will name things in Latin America, not so that Europe will recognize it but for our own inventory. Sábato and Galeano are the bridge builders. Marta Traba in her *Homérica Latina* is possessed by the multitude and through her voice an entire people speaks, the shapeless and disheveled masses who bear the burden of all the calamities and papal benedictions, the cannon fodder. That is why today, at least in México, the chronicle is so widespread because in it people like Carlos Monsiváis, José Joaquín Blanco, Saborit y Bellinhausen, Pérez Gay and Héctor Aguilar Camín gather the voices of everyone. The narrative substance is in all the voices, and by doing so they not only document what's going on in our country but also they construct our memory, because a people without memory is a people who haven't learned any lessons and who will unavoidably go back and commit the errors of their past.

Finally, despite the fact that our maps are no longer those of Spanish cosmographers, Latin America still has zones waiting to be discovered. We can name those ourselves, identify them ourselves, cultivate them ourselves, yank them out of solitude ourselves, bring them together ourselves. We have had great pioneers: Artigas, Gallegos, José Eustacio Rivera who galloped over vast plains, but essayists like Henríquez Ureña and Angel Rama were discovered also. In Latin America today, millions and millions of Latin Americans—subjected to the dominating violence which appropriated our natural resources—search for a new path, the path of America's own unity. To unite, not disappear, in order to end our exploitation (to support one another amongst ourselves and in the land's huge potential, to exploit on our own its abundant natural resources and to manufacture our own consumer goods). The liberation is common to all. We do not want to be peoples without memory. By uniting we don't invalidate ourselves, don't attenuate the character traits of any one individual. On the contrary, by solving the problems of our economy and technological backwardness, we will fertilize our garden, the common garden, that enormous continental garden, and then we will blossom.

Literature has given the examples through García Márquez and his Macondo. Our peoples are speaking through one voice, and the loves, the vengeances, the infidelities, the births and deaths become an epic poem, and we are all protagonists of this: the women who in harmony fly through the air grasping a sheet and the men who chisel little golden fish before going to battle. Together we weave our unity, the gigantic cloak over the shoulders of Bolívar.

Translated by Alan West.

ART AND IDENTITY IN LATIN AMERICA

RITA EDER

On a certain occasion, a Brazilian conceptual artist delivered a lecture in México City to an auditorium filled with young art students. To present his work he chose to emphasize the cultural differences between his country of origin and the country that welcomed him.

"In Brazil," he said, speaking with characteristic Brazilian eloquence, "we risk the ephemeral, the on-the-spot comment, the acid-like criticism, the ignoble materials, frivolity and transgression because we lack the presence of the eternal. Everything decays thanks to the violence of the elements: the sun, sea salt, humidity." (The artist was originally from Rio de Janeiro.) "But," he continues, "Mexico is made of stone. Nothing disappears. Tradition has a powerful visual presence. There, in that dry *altiplano* rules the might of Teotihuacán, with its enormous pyramids, unimaginable minimalist sculptures, a challenge for any artist of our time. This partially explains why in Brazil a new art has developed, whereas México adheres to another rhythm which carries the imprint of memories."

I do not know if these were the exact words. Ten years have passed already and a lot more has been said on this topic, but I remember well that these were the essential concepts.

This audacious and somehow superficial assertion is, nonetheless, useful in order to introduce the proposed topic for this gathering. Every time that the issue of identity in Latin American visual arts is discussed, what is really on the table is the legitimacy, or the exercise of conceptualizing, the modern. So when a Brazilian artist differentiates between two opposed identities of the Latin American continent, what he is really saying is that Brazil, a country of immigrants joined together by a strong African presence and lacking a strong pre-Columbian or colonial cultural past, can allow itself to travel freely within the Western cultural legacy; whereas México belongs to another ethnic and cultural reality altogether, where modernity, in order to be, has to elaborate first on the presence of its past.

With this example we can notice, on one hand, the difficulties of speaking about a Latin American art with such a diverse cultural geography. On the other hand, lying at the heart of the controversy is the idea of rescuing the national spirit and the desire to belong freely to the contemporary universal art world.

In this paper I will outline some fundamental moments in the controversy regarding Latin American arts. If I resort to recent history, it is because the proposals stated during the nationalist years (1920-1940) are still valid as visual traditions. We'll see how the idea of a Latin American art was first based on the artistic movements and how later this concern depended more on its inclusion in institutions such as museums, biennales and galleries. This already indicates how the expansion of the art market has influenced this cultural history, and also indicates the need to be alert to these factors.

* * *

The contemporary debate on identity and visual arts in Latin America began in the early 1970s[1]. Certainly, this is a concern with a long trajectory, beginning in the late 19th century. Its most productive moments on the creative and intellectual levels occurred between 1920 and 1945, more or less, when the idea of the Latin American culture as a manifestation of an arriving political unification, already laid out by Martí and Vasconcelos, Mariátegui and Haya de la Torre and others, gained strength.

A quick analysis of the texts written by ideologues of Latin Americanism in the visual arts[2] shows the close relationship they found between the political factors, marked by colonialism, and the need for one's own cultural manifestation as a testimony to the liberation from European tutelage and as a protection against the growing imperialism over Latin America, all expressed with the self-assurance that comes from a messianic attitude. The new prophets of a continent were created, linked by the same history, the same language[3], and aiming to create an art different from that of Europe. It was a project inspired in formal roots, in lifestyles and in the daily life and the objects of the marginalized groups in Latin America.

The formulation of this aesthetic was influenced by the European discovery of the so-called "primitive art," by the English Arts and Crafts movement, and finally, in México, by the integration of popular art into the strict program of the so-called "fine arts."

There were at least four fundamental propositions, all different but all of them responding to the problem of how to express the spirit of this new legitimation of reality.

THE FOUR PROPOSITIONS

Mexican artists responded, in this case, to Vasconcelos' call as Minister of Education during the period of General Obregón, with the muralist movement, founded in 1922. Muralism placed as the central point of its imagery the articulation of a new history that would include the ordinary people as protagonists, ethnically and as a class. México's novel contribution was the breaking up of an aesthetic system and the creation of a new narrative intended for a different public.

The counterpoint of the Mexican movement was Brazilian modernism—in which a will to be modern in the visual arts was maintained, but at the same time the theme of the work incorporated an exuberant landscape, a fantastic flora, and elements of negritude. Modernism in painting was immersed in the anthropophagic philosophy of Oswaldo de Andrade, who developed the idea that the principal element in the composition of an aesthetic is the capacity and duty to be nourished from all cultures, and, by digesting those cultures, to create something new.

The only Americanist project, "Constructive Universalism," was formulated by the Uruguayan Torres García, using a visual language articulated by inscribed symbols in an emotional geometry which contained, ideally, the ancestral memory of all the possible meanings that matter to mankind.

During the beginning of the 1940s, a series of manifestations started to take shape in the Caribbean visual arts that contributed to a sense of identity linked to the conception of daily life which, according to Western eyes, has been classified as fantastic. For example, I refer to the work of Wifredo Lam, developed more fully after his return to Cuba in 1941 after a long stay in Europe, and to the discovery of Hyppolite in Haiti, who along with other Haitian painters developed the Naif school, immersed in the meanings of voodoo[4]. Both Lam and Hyppolite gained international prominence when they confronted Surrealism. Breton, when passing through México and the Antilles, tried to integrate them into this current, and included them in his anthology *Surrealism and Painting*[5].

Breton's texts don't explain the work's relationship to an American context. The delicate syncretism that sustains the images in Caribbean paintings is not explored. The important eruption of the theme of negritude—not anecdotally, but as an image, and as a cultural and formal substratum in Latin America—is left untouched[6].

The confrontation between European intellectual Surrealism and the certainty that in America this dimension was part of daily life was shown by Alejo Carpentier—when he speaks of magical realism, he considers not only literature but architecture as well; Carpentier's surprise arises from something he has called the "Third Style," or, the style of things that have no style[7]. He describes the continuous superimposition of elements that come together compositionally, and it is here that his appreciation of colonial architecture, specifically of the Baroque period, lies: "An angel and a maraca weren't new objects in themselves, but an angel playing the maraca in the tympanum of a church ignites something which had never been seen anywhere else."[8]

In his well-known prologue to *The Kingdom of This World,* Carpentier makes a series of comments that became fundamental for artistic consciousness in Latin America. He established a dialogue with Surrealism. He rejected Surrealist formulas—this desire to provoke the magical "to the hilt," and signalled the impotence of Europeans in approaching American reality; because ultimately they are disbelievers, "they won't bet their souls on the fearsome card of faith." Carpentier arrived at magical-realism through Latin America's history. He tells its miracles, its myths, its magic. "And that it's due to the virginity of its landscape, the formation, anthology and the Faustian presence of the Indians and the Blacks. Due to the revelation of its recent discovery, due to the fertile crossbreeding, America is far from depleting its wealth of mythologies."[9]

Magical realism is apparently an accessible proposition: "We only have to be inspired by reality." To a certain extent this could have been a panacea because, as Carpentier says, reality is unlimited. Only a few have broken through the barrier of the anecdotal to recreate this cohabitation of the fantastic immersed in daily life.

This conception of society, recurring in an overflow of fantasy as opposed to a rational system, has been fought against over time and with enormous conviction. Some consider magical-realism a harmful expression, to the extent that it could represent the symptom of living in pre-logical socities. To be plunged into the world of myths is, according to some, to be opposed to any notion of social change. Others have said that the introduction of a rational system of imagery, for example *geometrismo,* should be nurtured and supported because it stands for rationality and encourages a better explanation of reality[10].

This is the central theme of the debate over Latin American art and identity. This search for identity has sometimes led to the supremacy of one style over others. It has featured, in its different periods, social realism (with predictable themes), magical realism, the combination of modern styles with a symbolic referent from the mythic realm, or a rationalist *geometrismo,* playful or symbolic. This way of stating the problem of Latin American art means going from how the visual arts have developed to how they ought to be.

SECOND STAGE OF THE DEBATE

A lot has been written about the controversies, discucssions and cultural actions produced between 1920 and 1945. Our purpose has been to summarize some of the fundamental propositions that arose during this period and to pinpoint some basic questions that were raised. Finally, this period comes to us with a clear profile based on the modern tradition of visual arts in Latin America.

Identity is an open concept. Therefore, what we ask ourselves today has to differ in its causes and responses from our immediate past. We can affirm that what we perceive as a novelty in this second approach to the topic is the need to question the concept of a Latin American art, and to conceptualize what we have called identity.

It was not in vain that a new inspection of Latin American art arose during the 1970s, after the furor caused by abstract art which, many believed, had come to stay. It was unimaginable to backpedal to a figurative art; and, more so, it was not yet imaginable to return to values with an external significance. This latter process took place mostly in México, after more than 30 years of dominance by the Mexican School, but we can also see it in Julio Le Parc. Argentina and Brazil, in contact with international art, overcame any localist connotation in order to be part of the new global scenario in the visual arts. The strict rules of Constructivism were the avenue that led to Venezuelan Modernism. We could say that the International Style obtained its more spectacular achievements in the works of Latin American architects and their flirtation with the integration of all the arts; Brasilia and the university cities of México and Carácas being the most obvious examples.

Latin American development in these countries, with their growth at any cost, has exposed the fallacy that a world in which access to goods would be for all is, in fact, the economic theory on which internationalism is based.

The desire to be modern triumphed, and being modern during the mid-seventies had a fundamental motivating factor—the creation of something new that looked ahead to a conception of the future—something that was very much encouraged in that period. For highly developed countries, this meant considering two questions which were gaining prominence in daily life: the advance of technology, and the strength of an urban culture abetted by publicity and the new visual habits of the masses.

How is one to deal with the orientation of Latin American or national plastic arts vis-a-vis the dilemma of newness and all that it entails? Responses were given by the Brazilian Ferreira Gullar in his paper *"Vanguard and Underdevelopment"*[11] and by Marta Traba, in *Two Vulnerable Decades of Latin American Art*[12]. Gullar embraces the new as catalyst for change in the world of underdevelopment. Traba, on the opposite side, maintains that the crucial issue is to resist the crunching influence of the vanguard and hold onto our own position, which would translate into the creation of icons symbolizing the mythic roots still alive in Latin American culture.

The concern which characterizes the periods of abundance, that of becoming internationals, was shattered with the different political changes that took place in Latin America. Among the strongest examples are the movement of 1968 in México, and the hardening of the military dictatorship in Argentina. This provoked a questioning of how the art world functions, including the role of exhibition spaces and of the public for whom the work is intended and, finally, questions about the purpose of art. In various countries a change was set in motion that brought about a real departure. The use of materials was re-evaluated. Graphic arts took over the preeminent position that had been allotted to painting. A direct message substituted for content that had been rich in ambiguity. Finally, the street was seen as a privileged scenario, favored over the relatively closed circles of museums and galleries. The artist's ambitions grew in such a way that they intended to seize consciousness or, at least, to stir it up.

In México there was the phenomenon of the "groups." In Argentina, various artistic "events" targeted disinformation[13]. Cuba, since the Revolution in 1959, had already been working in this direction, especially through posters, but it was an exceptional case in the Latin American panorama of the 1960s.

In the middle of this turn in artistic production, a crisis occurred that led to a questioning of the whole art world, and the question of identity emerged. I suspect that this debate arose due to a perceived loss of strength for Latin America and also due to an excess of confusion within the arts created by the disintegration of a language (which, until then, had been relatively precise), by introducing the concept of "actions" to replace "objects." This alarmed the art market, and provoked a genuine disorientation toward new artistic attitudes. On the other hand, it was a moment of new outlooks, since these events allowed an approach in which artists could begin anew.

As a response to this range of problems, the field of Latin American art presents, among others, the following concerns which, for reasons of clarity, we'll divide into categories.

COLONIALISM: INTERNAL AND EXTERNAL

Within the idea of a Latin American art there have been two basic tendencies, one metropolitan and the other Indo-Hispanic. The most relevant moments that stand out in Latin America's most prominent capitals took place in México, Brazil, Venezuela, Argentina, Colombia and, at times, Uruguay, leaving little room for smaller countries and non-indigenous ethnic minorities. Only recently has there been an insistence on the presence of Africa in Latin America, and perhaps this was the factor that unleashed the need to integrate the Caribbean as part of Latin America, in order to analyse problems as a whole. As René Depestre said; "Only an Americanology, without the Afro-, Indo-, or Euro-centric prefixes, will allow for the analysis and reevaluation of our sociocultural phenomena concerning a conceptual and methodological imperialism which has divided, dismembered, fractured, racialized and rationalized the knowledge of laws governing our history."[14] Depestre's idea is to promote a way of thinking which stresses a genuine and full American-ness, as a measure of political protection. The more fragmented Latin America is, the weaker it is in standing up to the U.S. In contrast, with regard to the colonialism that comes from abroad, there are those who say that there is a concrete problem for the arts *vis-a-vis* international art institutions such as biennales and prizes.

This idea stems from Brazil, which has always held an ecumenical approach, belonging by nature to the Western world. "Brazil can no more escape the Latin American contingency than other countries in the continent can exclude Brazil from their continental thinking. We should both develop the necessary theories capable of advancing our artistic production. Together we should promote our artists and the aesthetic born here, within and without the continent. Only then can we avoid the blockade by arts market multinationals and the colonization imposed by large international exhibits. We can resist or liberate, but we must resist with new languages or, better still, with the new. This is why we can devour everything useful for our need to express our being. We have been robbed and exploited enough. Art has served to oppress us and biennales try to do the same: they are the new instruments of defining what is art."[15]

UNITY OR DIVERSITY

In relation to Latin American and Caribbean unity *vis-a-vis* culture and particularly art, the need has been to break this unitary concept since, basically, Latin America is rich in regionalisms. There are enormous differences in lifestyles, practices and customs. We can see this in the cultural manifestations and in the objects produced, in geographical differences and in the different ethnic groups. Each symbolic system is underlined by persisting regionalisms, still untouched by the concept of national unity. We can observe this to a greater extent as we relate one Latin American country to another and compare their visual arts, for example. This thesis maintains that in order to extrapolate characteristics for Latin American art (globally) we should first bring out the particularities akin to each country and undertake comparative studies. Until this happens, the concept of Latin Americanism in art will have no solid basis.

The interest in formulating these problems as a whole lies in the ability to build a reference plane for the discussion of common problems, which sometimes have nothing to do with the art world itself, but with what lies outside of the domain of art such as the institutions, the spaces and the reception process. There are basically two unifying instances when we can properly speak of a Latin American art. First of these are the images that arose in accepting and assimilating the elements of nationalism. Second are those artistic manifestations which began during the 1970s which, because they didn't concentrate on producing objects but instead on the arena of social action and linkage to social movements, were able to become something beyond art. And regarding these, Latin America has its own causes, its own struggles. We have already gone beyond the idea or barrier that images either represent reality or are simply icons of social life.

IDENTITY

The word identity is constantly found in passages of our literature that try to reclaim cultures peripheral to the Western world, especially in the visual arts. This is because, until this century, to make images in the fine arts sense was strictly dictated by European standards. This situation was modified when the legitimation of pre-Columbian cultures burst onto the stage, even more forcefully than the discovery itself.

It is necessary to question the concept of identity when we speak of it concerning Latin American art. In general terms, we have implicitly understood the concept as a way to set apart from or detect, so to speak, those characteristic qualities or particularities that make our visual expressions different from the international avant-garde. Identifying what makes us different entails an affirmation, not only of the originality of our contributions to the visual arts, but also a revelation of a path for other generations to follow. This doesn't exclude the problem of distinctiveness between Latin American countries themselves. Then it becomes clear that identity is used in two senses: as all that which differentiates Latin American visual arts from the metropolitan centers of art and, at the same time, the urgency to think through the extent to which one Latin American country is different from another and, therefore, the difficulty of finding identical characteristics.

To ask oneself about identity is not only an expression of doubt as to whether we are different or not, but also of how we are different. What underlies this statement is the issue of cultural colonization and the devaluation it imposes on us. The concept of identity has been analyzed by historians and theorists. For some, this proposition is totally erroneous, insofar as denoting a unitary identity of Latin American art implies finding common features among countries so absolutely divergent. They opt instead for the concept of entity, related to a geographical-political context and not necessarily to a commonality in cultural characteristics.

In addition to all the definitions that can be given to the concept of identity, there is a fundamental underlying question from psychology: who am I? Therefore, maybe it is more useful to connect identity not to a psycho-social concept but to an ensemble of ideas and beliefs (which, of course, change) which an identity has about itself. In some way, to speak about identity is to speak about ideology, not a false consciousness, but as this vast set of ideas and beliefs that a people practice in relation to itself and that are always changing.

FINAL CONSIDERATIONS

Clearly, there is a vast task ahead of us. There is no single text, as in literature, which brings together all the complexities inherent in the propositions put forth by the visual arts, within the wide frame of what is Latin American. There already exists a history of artistic production, an elaboration of an aesthetic congruent to Latin America's reality. There is also progress in the relation between social history and the formation of images. However, our relation to foreign conceptions is still pending. How do we fit in an aesthetic system created for European art? How has the U.S. overcome this situation?

At the heart of this debate about identity is the problem of legitimacy. Is there enough quality in Latin American art to place it in the international sphere? On the one hand, they accuse us of being regionalists and on the other, of being too similar to others and lacking originality. Self-discovery depends on us, otherwise we will depend on what is trendy; for example, whether primitive art is in vogue, or whether the Latino minority's votes are needed, or whether the meanings of representational art are of greater interest today than pure painting.

In two years there has been an avalanche of Latin American exhibits, and there are still more programmed for 1989 and 1990. Also two years ago, as we gathered at the Third World Biennale in Havana, we complained about the expulsion of Latin American art throughout the last several years from museums and biennales in the U.S. and various European countries. It could be interesting to figure out what motivates this dynamic, these abrupt changes in temperature. Today it is less possible than ever to separate oneself from the complex web that includes exhibiting spaces, market forces and the political motives that institutions, at certain moments, wield to favor art from the poor countries. Is it only a question of style or is it a realignment of power in the Western world?

Translated by Cristina Cardalda and Alan West.

NEW FORMS: CENTRAL AMERICA AND THE CARIBBEAN

OUR LITTLE REGION

CLARIBEL ALEGRIA

Mexican dictator Porfirio Díaz lamented at the turn of the century that his country was "so far from God and so close to the United States." The Central American and Caribbean nations have had excellent reasons to echo the same complaint for at least the same length of time. This closeness to the United States has determined—I would rather say deformed—national identities in the region ever since Teddy Roosevelt charged up San Juan Hill waving his saber, subsequently "took" Panama away from Colombia and finally added the Roosevelt corollary to the Monroe Doctrine.

For the past 90 years there has not been a single country in the area that has been exempt from U.S. pressures and manipulations, and there have been few that have escaped outright military intervention—always in the name of democracy. From the Spanish-American-Cuban War to 1920 alone, the United States intervened militarily in Honduras five times, in Nicaragua and the Dominican Republic four times, in Colombia, Panama, Cuba and Mexico three times and in Haiti twice.

Contrary to its proclaimed lofty and democratic intentions, the United States government has invariably intervened on behalf of

U.S. business interests and local oligarchies, and to uphold anachronistic and unjust political systems against any attempts at democratic reform or revolutionary change. The United States is a status quo power, and ever since the "Spanish-American" War, it has policed its Western Hemisphere bailiwick to preserve things as they are in countries that are crying out for social and political change. This has been the overriding reality throughout the area for almost the past 100 years, and without an understanding of this basic fact, one can understand nothing about Central America and the Caribbean nor the historical reasons for the popular anti-*yanqui* sentiment that pervades the region.

I grew up in a Central American "banana republic" that was largely exempt from direct U.S. intervention because it specialized in coffee and thus escaped the attention of the United Fruit Company. Yet U.S. warships stood by off the Salvadoran coast, ready to offer assistance, while a newly-installed dictatorship consolidated its power by slaughtering 30,000 peasants in the name of anti-communism. I was seven years old at the time, and I remember with hard-edged clarity when groups of them, their crossed thumbs tied behind their backs, were herded into the National Guard fortress just across the street from my house, and I remember the *coup de grace* shots startling me awake at night. Two years later, in 1934, I remember just as clearly my father, a Nicaraguan exile, telling me how Anastasio Somoza, with the benediction of the Yankee minister Arthur Bliss Lane had assassinated Sandino the night before.

I left El Salvador to attend a U.S. university; I married, had children and wrote poetry, convinced that Central American and Caribbean dictators—Martínez, Ubico, Carias, Somoza, Trujillo, Batista, Duvalier—were as inevitable and irremediable as the earthquakes, volcanic eruptions and electrical storms that scourge my homeland.

Thirty years ago, the Cuban revolution demonstrated that social and political change was possible in Latin America, but surely the Yankees with their helicopter gunships and Green Berets would never permit such a thing to happen again. Nevertheless, Fidel and Ché Guevara sensitized me to the currents of militant unrest just below the surface of the American *mare nostrum* in the Caribbean. My husband and I watched the eddies and whirlpools from

Paris and later from Mallorca while I nursed my growing burden of middle-class guilt. What was I doing sitting on the sidelines while my people silently suffered the implacable repression of the Somoza dynasty in Nicaragua and the rotating colonel-presidents in El Salvador? Some of my poems departed from the lyrical navel-gazing and nostalgia for my Central American childhood that had characterized my earleir work and began to focus on the misery, injustice and brutal repression that existed in my country.

Paris in the early 1960s was a meeting place for writers who were to make up the Latin American boom: Julio Cortázar, Mario Vargas Llosa, Carlos Fuentes and others. Inevitably we gravitated together and formed a nucleus of a sort of happy-go-lucky Mafia that Carlos Fuentes baptized as the Latin Cosa Nostra. We were attentive to the Cuban experiment, the CIA's thwarted Bay of Pigs invasion, the U.S. economic blockade. Latin American politics took its place alongside literature as a principal preoccupation. At the same time, my own childhood memories became a haunting obsession and I would tell friends anecdotes about my early youth in Santa Ana. It was Carlos Fuentes who urged me to plunge into the deep waters of the novel.

"I couldn't possibly," I protested. "I don't have the mental organization to write a novel."

"Let's write it together," my husband volunteered, and the result was *Ashes of Izalco,* a historical novel based on the events of 1932, which today—inexplicably—is a required high school text in El Salvador.

In 1966 we moved to Mallorca and settled in Deya, a marvelous little village enfolded between pine and olive-covered mountains and the wine-dark Mediterranean. The next 12 years were tranquil and productive. I continued to concentrate on my poetry, but I also found time to finish two novellas and a number of translations.

It was the taking of the National Palace in Managua and the insurrection of 1978 that rekindled my obsession with Central American politics. My husband and I began writing newspaper and magazine articles about the incandescent situation in the area. I remember that one of these articles, which dealt with the heroic figure of Archbishop Oscar Arnulfo Romero, was published at the beginning of 1979 in the Mexican newspaper Unomásuno under the prophetic headline "Murder in the Cathedral."

We followed the final Nicaraguan insurrection of June-July 1979 step by step and, two days before Somoza fled to Miami, my husband proposed that we travel to Nicaragua to write a book about the revolution. I accepted unhesitatingly, and a few weeks later we found ourselves surrounded by the devastation occasioned by the bloody struggle to bring down Somoza and his praetorian National Guard. This was another turning point in my life, and our book, *NICARAGUA: The Sandinista Revolution,* was printed in México a year or so later.

We lived for six months in Nicaragua, gathering material and testimonies for the book and then we returned to Mallorca to do the actual writing. On our way back we passed through Paris and a student group at the Sorbonne asked me to give a talk on the political situation in El Salvador. The day before I was scheduled to speak, Archbishop Romero was shot through the heart while saying mass, by cohorts of Roberto d'Aubuisson. We stayed up most of the night writing a new text that tried to evaluate the life and work of the only Salvadoran figure of international prestige who had served as the sole voice of the millions of voiceless in my homeland. In response to his brutal and tragic martyrdom, all but two or three of El Salvador's artists and intellectuals made the quiet decision, without so much as consulting each other, to do what we could to try to fill the enormous vacuum left by his death.

Since then, I have found myself writing more and more poems and prose texts that reflect the prevailing realities in my homeland. I have never deliberately set out to write a political poem, and I am fully aware of the pitfalls of trying to defend a transient political cause in what presumes to be a literary work. Political concerns do have a way of creeping into my poetry, however—simply because the Central American situation is one of my major obsessions, and I have always written poetry under obsession's spur. I personally prefer to think of my political poems as love poems directed to my country and my people, but I realize that this is begging the question and that there is a real artistic and aesthetic problem involved.

I have tried to resolve the dilemma, not by denying myself the right to deal with political themes, but by trying to be especially self-critical whenever I happen to produce a political poem. Secondly, I have deliberately divided my writing into two separate compartments. The first might be called the "literary-poetic," if you will, while the other is what I have come to think of as my "crisis journalism." An unkind critic might call it pamphleteering, I suppose, but I am not ashamed to produce a book, an article or a speech that openly defends a cause or situation in which I deeply believe.

I deeply believe in the Sandinista revolution, for instance, just as I believe in the historical necessity for a thorough political revolution in my own country, El Salvador, and I do my best to defend these two causes whenever I have the opportunity to do so. The present moment is one such occasion, inasmuch as I have been asked to address myself to the problem of Central America and the Caribbean and to say something about my own writing as well. Those of you who have been following my words will note how skillfully I have converted this literary forum into a political platform, and as you watch me now you will see how casually I doff my "literary-poetic" hat and don my pamphleteering hat.

The blood-drenched reality of Central America over the past two decades has been such a traumatic spectacle that no self-respecting human being in the area can avoid taking sides. Any artist who avoids commitment in this struggle is guilty at least of ivory tower escapism and at worst of complicity with the Squadrons of Death and the total militarization of society.

The principal cause of the chaos and bloodshed in Central America has been President Reagan's heavy-handed intervention in every country in the region over the past eight years in a misguided attempt to reestablish U.S. hegemony over what it has arrogantly labeled its "backyard." His policies have failed, his interventions have backfired and he has done more to destabilize the entire area and to create enduring enmity toward the United States than the Cubans and Soviets could possibly have achieved had they been permitted a free hand in the area for the same length of time. Let us take a brief look at what eight years of the Reagan Doctrine have wrought in Central America:

In El Salvador the FMLN[1] is stronger and more united than ever, and is operating in every province of the country. The doctrine of Low Intensity Conflict has failed miserably for the simple reason that you cannot create widows and orphans one day and "win their hearts and minds" by returning to offer them beans and candy bars the next. The mass movements which were virtually decimated in 1980 and 1981 are regaining their previous strength and fearlessness, and the pressures of hunger, unemployment and population growth are recreating a pre-insurrectional situation which could well reach the combustion point if Roberto d'Aubuisson's Death Squad party, ARENA, wins the next elections, as it may very well do[2]. Duarte is departing the scene, his Christian Democratic Party is divided and has lost the labor union support it once had, and is discredited nationally because of massive corruption by its leading figures.

We turn next to Nicaragua where, to use several of President Reagan's pet expressions, the "totalitarian Communist dictatorship" of the Sandinistas has for seven years successfully withstood the dedicated democratizing efforts of his valiant "freedom fighters," whom he equates with the "Founding Fathers of the Republic." Just to set the record straight one more time, Nicaragua is not and never was a totalitarian Communist dictatorship, and Mr. Reagan's freedom fighters are a gang of thugs, rapists and murderers who are intent on re-establishing a Somoza-style dictatorship, without Somoza. This, the Nicaraguan people will never permit, and there are 200,000 rifles in the hands of the people to guarantee that the National Guard will never again take control of the bunker above Tiscapa[3]. The Contras themselves are divided and quarrelling over the remaining spoils of the U.S. aid package, while the internal political parties are apparently more interested in dancing to the tune of their CIA puppet masters than in developing political platforms that might successfully compete with the Sandinistas—although the latter have pre-empted most of the political high ground.

In Guatemala, General Romeo Lucas García initiated a bloodbath in 1980 when the guerrilla movement spread to indigenous groups in the highlands. President Reagan renewed military aid to Guatemala in June 1981, although the bulk of counter-insurgency arms and training was provided by Israel. In March 1982, General Efrain Rios Montt, a born-again Evangelist, came to power through a coup and, with the encouragement of the White House, waged a genocidal, scorched-earth wipeout of hundreds of Indian villages. No one knows how many thousands were killed, but an estimated half million persons were displaced, and about 200,000 of these fled to Mexico and Honduras. Having established this sepuchral peace, the Guatemalan army in November 1985 permitted the election of Vinicio Cerezo, a Christian Democrat, as President. This apparently ended a long line of military dictators, but Cerezo himself after his inauguration admitted that he was serving only on the sufferance of the army.

Honduras, as we all know, has been turned into a U.S. aircraft carrier and military base aimed at Nicaragua, and a sanctuary for the Contras. Although the Honduran armed forces have benefitted from U.S. military aid, the rest of the economy remains sunk in stagnation, and the U.S. overlordship plus the Contra presence has created growing resentment among Honduran nationalists.

Costa Rica, with the highest per capita debt in the hemisphere, is another hostage to Mr. Reagan's Central America policy. President Arias and his predecessors have been forced to relinquish effective control of their northern border to the CIA and the Contra forces of ARDE[4]. U.S. efforts to militarize Costa Rica have been partially successful, and paramilitary squads are sprouting in a nation that disbanded its army 40 years ago.

Finally, we come to Panama, site of the strategic inter-ocean passageway and headquarters of the Southern Command which has played a crucial role in Mr. Reagan's counter-insurgency program over the past eight years. Recently we have been watching the Reagan administration's ludicrous and unavailing efforts to topple General Noriega. His own people and other Central American observers refuse to get excited about the drug-trafficking charges against Noriega, which are a transparent subterfuge to eliminate a troublesome patriot and nationalist who insists that the terms of the Torrijos-Carter agreement be observed, and that Panama assume full control of the Canal by the year 2000.

The United States has been transformed into an outlaw nation by the Reagan administration. It has repeatedly violated the U.N. and O.A.S. charters, and defies a ruling by the International Court of Justice that it cease its aggression against Nicaragua. It continues to foment war rather than peace in Central America. To paraphrase the title of this gathering, I can assure my listeners that Central America is awakening and that this awakening is in large measure an enraged reaction to an American administration that has gone out of its way to reconfirm the worst of the old clich*es about big stick and gunboat diplomacy and ugly Americans. To conclude, I wish you well in your forthcoming presidential elections, and I fervently pray that you do better next time.

(August 1988)

Translated by D. J. Flakoll

QUESTIONS FROM THE AUDIENCE

Question: What role is Vinicio Cerezo, the señor presidente of Guatemala, playing, since he is also a puppet of the United States, retained by the United States—or do you have a different opinion?

CA: I find that Vinicio Cerezo is not as dependent on the U.S. as, for example, Duarte or Azcona, but yes, in certain ways he is dependent. As he himself has said, he is governing with the consent of the army, and everybody knows that the Guatemalan army is dependent on the United States. So, in one way or another, he is also...

Question: Knowing what has always been the case of elections held in Central America, could you tell us what is the position being taken by revolutionary groups in Central America, most especially in El Salvador, now that elections are approaching?

CA: Well, I will speak in concrete terms about El Salvador. Elections in El Salvador have always been fraudulent. In past years, for example, after Martínez and all the colonels, one after the other; imagine that they carried people, the farm workers, in trucks [to the polling places]. The owners of the plantations did this. So, now we will see what happens in these new elections. I suppose they will be fraudulent also. For example the parties of the FDR (Frente Democratico Revolucionario[5]) of El Salvador want to enter the elections. We'll see if they get cheated or not, and we are going to see whether they are really allowed to participate, and if everyone is allowed to vote. For example, people living in the zones controlled by the FMLN and FDR have not been allowed to vote up to now. And what is that, except a big fraud?

Question: A question from the art world. As an admirer of the poetical work of Claribel Alegría, I would like to ask you what has been the impact in Nicaragua and the rest of Central America of the Sandinista revolution, in terms of cultural expression and the arts?

CA: It has been very large, because you know that with the triumph, Ernesto Cardenal, who was then Minister of Culture in Nicaragua, created what is called the studios, or workshops, of poetry. They were set up throughout the country, and in addition gave an impetus to cultural magazines like *Nicaraguac,* for example, or *La Revista de Poesía,* or the weekly supplements of the newspapers *Ventana* and the *Nuevo Amanecer Cultural.* And despite the dictatorships in the rest of Central America, these publications have slipped through, some reaching El Salvador, Honduras, Guatemala—and have had a big impact. And one more thing (not to go on too long, since I can talk for hours about all of this); in Nicaragua, they are very generous, and so not only do they publish Nicaraguan poets, but other Latin American poets, particularly those from other Central American countries, so their writers can become known there.

Question: You spoke of the fact that the government is doing many things to erase the popular history of El Salvador. However your book *Ashes of Izalco,* which describes the massacre of 1932, is now required reading in the country's public schools. This is an extraordinary thing; how do you explain it?

CA: Yes, it's incredible. The book was first published in Spain in 1966. Ten years passed before it was known in El Salvador, in the first place because my family burned almost all of the first edition because they didn't like what I said about their social class, about them. Well, then, after 1976, when Molina was dictator of El Salvador, just as he was about to leave, he wanted to go out as a great liberal. He said that he wanted all the Salvadoran writers to be included in the publications of the Ministry of Culture. So they published it, without reading it, naturally, and they classified it as a textbook because the title itself does speak of El Salvador. And since then, I am sure that because they see the seal of the Ministry of Culture, they keep it. I imagine it has sold a lot of copies, since it has gone through some 20 editions. And not only that, but they read it in prisons. The book will come out in English next year.

Translated by Cola Franzen.

FIRST PERSON SINGULAR?

NORBERTO JAMES

I come from the Dominican Republic, a country that can claim the dubious honor of five interventions into its internal affairs by the United States. As a poet, literary critics agree that I am to be found among the poets and critics who came of age during and after the military occupation of 1965.

When any North American of approximately my age recalls with particular enthusiasm the experiences of their lives in the Sixties, I can identify with their peculiar passion, given my own experience. It was a time of profound, personal definitions. I defined my identity, my sense of self as a Dominican. I made a conscious effort to value my heritage as a descendant of "cocolo" immigrants, a fact that I will try to explain further on. I published my first book, *On The March,* and I set myself the goal of getting a university education.

The regime of Rafael Leonidas Trujillo was a dictatorship which subjugated the Dominican people for thirty years, from 1930-1960. By serving the United States as well as the Dominican oligarchy, Trujillo had the peculiarity, typical of Third World dictators, of using political power to gain personal wealth for himself, his family and his friends. On May 30, 1960, with a green light from the State Department of the United States, Trujillo was assassinated by his closest collaborators.

In 1962 the first free elections were held. The Dominican people voted for Juan Bosch, thereby frustrating plans made in Washington which had counted on a victory by the candidate most favorable to U.S. interests. For this reason Juan Bosch presided over a government that was stillborn, in power only long enough to oversee the creation and approval of the most democratic Constitution in our history: the Constitution of 1963, which failed to become law due to the intervention of the United States in 1965 and the subsequent military occupation of the country.

Once the deed was done, Lyndon B. Johnson informed the American people that he had resorted to such a measure because "what had begun as a popular and democratic revolution had fallen into the hands of the communists." To justify such an atrocity, someone in Washington came up with the idea of the now famous list of 58 communists, which was made available to the international press. The list included names of individuals who were still in exile, in jail or even dead. Days later, the "Ministry of North American Colonies," as we used to call it, better known as the Organization of American States, gave its blessing to the occupation by approving an American proposal to create the Fuerza Interamericana de Paz (Interamerican Peace Force).

United States troops remained in Dominican territory until after the elections of 1966. The candidate of the invading forces, Joaquín Balaguer, our present Dominican President, was the victor. What followed was a period of modernization for Dominican society which resulted in the reinforcement of oligarchic power and a greater dependency on the United States.

The use of violence was put into practice as a main instrument of the government. During the following 12 years (1966-1978), everyday life was marked by incidents of torture, deportation and death, anything and everything that the regime deemed useful in its effort to contain expression by the opposition.

Literary production during the months of the occupation was characterized by a commitment to oppose these political circumstances, and by its capacity to bear witness and to chronicle events. The cultural organizations that we began to create (The Fist, The Island, The Torch and The Mask) were a reflection not only of class stratification in our society, but also of the atomization of our political organizations.

The group "El Puño" (The Fist) described itself as a group of writers and artists committed to their people and to their time. The core members of the group "La Isla" wanted to be more specific. In 1969, in the prologue to my first book, Antonio Lockward, the mentor of the group, sketched out what would become the fundamental points of our Declaration of Principles. We established that we would fight for the independence of the Dominican Republic, for the democratization of education in order to defend our progressive cultural heritage and for the creation of a realistic approach to art.

I arrived at poetry by way of the April War. It was during the development of this event that I managed to get to know a good number of people who were to be my friends and allies in groups and political activities.

During my childhood and part of my adolescence, English was my language of expression. My grandmother, Marion Petters, an illiterate woman, a sweet, strict and religious *mulatta* from the island of Dominica, restricted me from any contact with the Spanish-speaking population. She had her reasons. "You're not a Dominican," she would say, "Take a look at our two last names: James Rawlings. Besides, I don't want them to call you 'cocolo.' "

In the Dominican Republic, the word "cocolo" had strong negative and racist connotations. During the Haitian occupation from 1822 to 1844, it was used in reference to the troops from the neighboring republic. The establishment of the sugar industry in the country, at the beginning of the century, attracted a wave of immigrants from the Caribbean Basin, most of them black, who spoke little Spanish. As a good number of them came from the island of Tortola, they came to be known as "cocolos." This is the argument offered by some historians. Nevertheless I have no doubt that, since our people share the same skin color as that of the Haitians, and since, in a like manner, we were perceived as usurpers of jobs in the industry, the term was applied to us with the same racist and derogatory intent.

With the fall of the Trujillo regime, many of these workers returned to their native countries, and that closed community into which I had been born and raised dispersed, just when I became

First Person Singular?

aware of my repressed identity. I do not know if it is unfair to say that it was only after the success of my poem "The Immigrants" that the contribution of this community was objectively and fairly appreciated. In order not to take sides in offering a description of this community, I would like to quote the historian Fernando Pérez Memén:

> "The "cocolos" constitute a positive immigration. Their ordered life. Their austere and disciplined habits. Their honesty and hard-working nature are virtues of which they may be proud. (...) Many bring honor to the country with their talents as notable educators, prominent doctors, religious ministers, engineers, chemists, administrators and outstanding athletes."

During the years preceding the publication of my first book, I managed to pass the test as a poet by getting my poems published, as was customary, in the cultural supplements of the most prestigious newspapers in the country.

In 1969, I won a prize in one of the most important literary contests of that period, from the Autonomous University of Santo Domingo, with the poem "The Immigrants," written in homage to my forebears.

As a third generation "cocolo," I lived through and freed myself from the economic and intellectual slavery that my parents experienced and experience to this day. The trauma of the military occupation in 1965, and the consequent frustration of the April Revolution, made it all the more urgent for me to define my identity. I felt the moment had come to reclaim for myself and for them the place which we had earned for ourselves as a part of the Dominican people. This claim was raised in the following poem:

The Immigrants

The story of their sorrow
Is not yet written.
Their old pain joined to ours.

Norberto James

   They had no time
—as children—
to seize between their fingers
the multiple colors of butterflies
to fix their eyes on the landscapes of the archipelago
to know the humid song of the rivers.

   They had no time to say:
—This land is ours.
We'll gather colors.
Make a flag.
Defend her.

   There was a time
—I never knew—
when the cane
the millions
and the province with an Indian name
brackish and wet
had its own music
and from the most remote places
the dancers would come.

Because of the cane
the sea
the cold winding rail
many were trapped.
Left behind the merry flight of others
remained only the sound of the name untouched
difficult to pronounce
the decrepit town
the dusty barrio
noiselessly crumbling
the pathetic inertia of the carriage horse
the youth, clubbed and beaten
needing
the warmth of his true country.

First Person Singular?

The ones who remained. These.
The ones with blurred smiles
lazy tongues
weaving the sounds of our language
are
the firm root of my forebears
old rock
where the ancient hatred of the crown
of the sea
of this horrible darkness
plagued by monsters
grows and burns furiously.
Hey there old Willy coachman
faithful lover of masonry.
Hey you George Jones
unwearying bicycle rider
John Thomas preacher.
Whinston Brodie teacher.
Prudy Ferdinand trumpet player.
Cyril Chalenger railroad engineer
Aubrey James chemist.
Violeta Stephen soprano.
Chico Conton baseball player.

I come with all the old drums
bows arrows
wooden swords and axes
painted in all colors
dressed up
in the many colored costume of Primo
the Goliath Dancer-nurse.

I come to write your names
next to the others
to offer you
this land, mine and yours
because you earned it
by our side
in the daily struggle

for bread and peace
for light and love.
Because every day that passes
every day that falls
upon your tired worker's salt
we build
the light that you want for us
we secure
the possibility of the song
for all.

The poets of my group used to say in verses what the newspapers would refuse to say in print. In other words, our conception of literature was and is, I should say, that literature is an instrument that should be useful to the process of urgent social change in our society. That position made us deserving of labels like propagandists, pamphleteers, agitators, etc.

Personally I took these labels very seriously, given my academic background back then. At that time, I had not been able to complete my secondary education. But the constant work in the study groups of La Isla, the deep personal existential crisis that I was going through, in addition to the selective and systematic killings carried out by the administration of Joaquín Balaguer, precipitated my decision to realize my dream of getting an academic education.

In 1972, I published my second book, *The Province in Revolt*, a book of poems that moved away from the direct denunciations of my first book. Here the poems become shorter in length. I began to work more carefully. That same year, thanks to the generosity of the people and the government of Cuba, I received a scholarship from the University of Havana so that I could begin my university studies.

According to some critics, the group of poets to which I belong fell "victim" to freedom of expression. We feel that we fulfilled our obligation regardless, at a moment in history which called for the kind of poetic discourse that we embarked upon. The group of poets that came before us, under the dictatorship, had to resort to a cryptographic poetic discourse. In us, voices that had been repressed during 30 years of dictatorship broke out in a stampede. It is true that we called everything by its name in a direct manner. It is certain that, in a few cases, that way of working poetic material was detrimental to a few. It was also true that my group was poorly educated. It should be said, however, that it is the only one in our history of letters in which the majority of us have gone on to receive degrees in literature. It should also be known that we are the only group in Dominican letters that has reflected critically on its own body of work, in at least three anthologies. Some students of Dominican literature characterize us as a "generation with no teachers." More appropriate, if a label is necessary, would be "the self-taught generation," which fits the facts more closely.

During the 12 years of the Balaguer regime, those of us who as writers and artists came of age during the April Revolution in 1965 ended up following very different paths. Most of us fell into a long silence. Some of us never published again. Of those in the group El Puno, many went into advertising, and had little or no time left for literary creation. Those of us from the groups La Isla and La Antorcha went back to university classrooms, some as students, others as professors, and at least in one case, suicide seemed to be the most viable solution to so much despair, so much frustration.

QUESTIONS FROM THE AUDIENCE

Question from Claribel Alegría about the racial situation in the Dominican Republic at the moment.

NJ: We Dominicans have the strange characteristic of not wanting to talk about the racial problem because to speak of it would be to discover that we are all black. There is a very folkloric saying in the Dominican Republic that "we all have some black behind the ear." I believe the best way of explaining the racial problem in the Dominican Republic is to see a group of Dominicans together, and we can see if we are or are not an eminently mulatto nation. What has happened is that historically, the ruling classes have wished to be enemies of the Haitian people solely on the basis of color, because really there is no great difference between Haitians and Dominicans. They are two peoples who occupy the geographical space of an island, who have shared the same historical trajectory and, therefore, I do not see what the difference is. There is no specific historical event that could separate us.

In essence, the Dominican people are a mulatto people. And it makes no sense for us to embark on a war without quarter, to stick a black label on the Haitians and an Indian label on the Dominicans. Certainly what has caused this laughter [heard in the audience] is the fact that there are Dominicans in the audience, and Dominicans know that someone of my color is called "dark Indian." Recently the passport division started officially to designate a person of my color as *"trigueño,"* "dark-complexioned."

Question: What has been the impact, in literary expression, of the exploitation and dehumanization of the Haitian workers, the cane cutters? Have artists denounced that dehumanization and exploitation?

NJ: Unfortunately, there are no texts in Dominican literature that take on that aspect of the problem. The people who have concerned themselves exclusively with such matters have been the historians and sociologists. Now in the area of the plastic arts— the painters, photographers, sculptors—yes, they have indeed done some effective work in denouncing that situation of slavery of the Haitian workers in the Dominican cane fields. Why have the writers not done so? That is a question that would have to be posed in the Dominican context. When such work has been done, it has been a caricature, to make fun of Haitians who speak Spanish with that accent...

Question: We are talking here of how, in Santo Domingo, there is racism against Haitians, and that people do not talk of how Haitians have been treated in the sugar mills. I would also like us to speak about the Haitians, about how, when they took up arms [against us], many Dominicans died in that war, and that the Dominicans had a right to live on their side of the island, according to a treaty that was in effect. That is, we had no problem; we lived on this side of the island, and the Haitians on the other. Then

First Person Singular?

they occupied our territory, took possession of our land. We were left without our territory. So I would like that also to be cleared up, not only "oh the poor Haitian, the poor things."

NJ: Very well. This question you have just posed fits like a glove because you have just expressed the official version of Dominican history. It is not the version that fits the events. Unfortunately, your being a young man,—I felt very sad while you were asking your question, to see how vehemently you express a position on Dominican history that is absolutely reactionary and that I know you do not share. So therefore I recommend to you that you read Emilio Cordero Michel's "La revolucion haitiana en Santo Domingo," so that you can understand why the ruling classes teach us to hate the Haitians for the occupation of the island from 1822 to 1844. Perhaps if you read the book you will also realize that Dominican independence would not have been possible without the aid of the Haitians who founded their republic, gaining their independence in 1804, much earlier than we did.

Perhaps you don't know this because you are very young. Maybe you also don't know that, during the North American intervention in 1965, it was the Haitians who helped us repair arms during the fight against the reactionary forces of Wessin in Santo Domingo. So I believe eventually you are going to revise your position.

Translated by Beth Wellington.

PLASTIC ARTS IN CUBA[1]

GERARDO MOSQUERA

In factories and other work places in Cuba, the fulfillment of work plans is usually celebrated in so-called "cultural/political activities." These activities have two parts: the political, which consists of speeches and the reading of reports; and, the cultural, which usually consists of dancing and beer drinking. As Claribel Alegría has taken charge of the political part, I can concentrate on the cultural aspects, even though I'm sure that it won't be as much fun as in Cuba. Of course, to set apart the cultural from the political is not really possible anywhere. My purpose is to focus on some internal problems of culture in a Latin American socialist country by looking at its visual arts.

Cuba is a strange place. It is the only socialist country in the Western Hemisphere, and on top of that it is only 45 minutes away from Miami by plane. At Guantánamo Bay, only a fence sets us apart from the United States, which seized a piece of our island. Cuba is also an archipelago, and its countryside is almost like that of the state of Virginia. (Maybe the people of Langley devote so much of their attention to us because of this coincidence.) It is an underdeveloped agricultural country without any significant natural resources. There are no energy sources, nor hydraulic

Plastic Arts in Cuba

wealth; our subsoil is poor, except for some nickel deposits, but unfortunately mining this ore requires a complex technological process which demands huge investments. To a large extent, Cuba still depends on sugar, and continues supplying socialist and Third World calories to a large part of humanity. Tourism has been successfully developed in the last few years.

Although it is the only country in the Western Hemisphere that is a member of CMEA (Council of Mutual Economic Assistance), Cuba is fully part of the Third World and is actively involved with countries of the Non-Aligned Movement. In official rhetoric we use the terms "friendly countries" and "brother countries." In my own judgement, I think we rather feel the socialist countries to be "friendly," and the Third World as "brother" countries. As part of a brotherhood of solidarity, we try to help the most unfortunate peoples with our "lonely widow's two coins," to paraphrase one of the many socialist passages of the Gospel.

Cuba is a Caribbean country where Hegel, besides having been stood on his head (as by Marx), has had to dance with abandon. It was not in vain that Ché Guevara, a man of the Southern Cone, spoke of a "socialism with *pachanga.*" Caribbean cultures are the outcome of the welding together of Western features (of European origin) and non-Western elements (of essentially African origin), in which the African elements have been a very active ingredient in art and literature. Even though Bastide[2] said that Cuba is the "whitest" among the Antilles, I think the African heritage comes out as being more internalized than obvious. But at the same time, in my native land African traditions are preserved with much purity. What's more, we export them, because Cuban emigration is making the *Yoruba* cult of the *Orishas* almost into a universal religion. Cuba is the only country of the African diaspora where there is a male secret society (a parastatal institution of social control typical of West Africa); the society of leopard men, with their masks and rituals. It is the only country where the *Ifá* divination system with its priests, the "fathers of secrets," is preserved, and the only place where the spirits of the dead work for their masters, who have made them prisoners inside the Kongo *nganga*[3] or *mpungu*[4], like genies in Aladdin's lamp. Not long ago Robert Farris Thompson was amazed by a sacred tree overflowing with offerings, a couple of blocks away from Revolution Square in Havana—

nothing noteworthy compared to a portrait of Lenin set upon an altar of *Ocha,* something surely too much for even Gorbachev to handle.

On the other hand Cuba was, except for Puerto Rico, the Latin American country subject to the greatest U.S. economic, political and cultural penetration from very early on. The Revolution put an end to this, but certain features persisted, like the baseball craze.

Cuban culture has always been very active, standing out over and above its material conditions. It is an open culture, restless in its avant-garde searchings and social concerns, and at times quite sophisticated. The visual arts, which happen to be my discipline, started their avant-garde period in the 1920s. Just as in other Latin American countries, artistic and literary vanguardism characteristically strengthened national identity and played a progressive role *vis-a-vis* social issues. This continued into post-Revolutionary society without interruption.

The complexities which I have outlined, together with many others, serve to demolish the clichés most often used whenever my homeland's present culture is observed from outside. In addition, the Revolution has carried forward the best cultural policy within the socialist community, a policy attuned to the unfolding of history and the realities of the country. Our culture has enjoyed a glasnost *avant la lettre.*

This policy is based on Fidel's well-known axiom; "Within the Revolution, everything. Against the Revolution, nothing." We haven't been made to suffer through an official art, nor to retaliate by way of an underground art, and recognition of artists has been based on the cultural worth of their work. Freedom of artistic creation is guaranteed in the very text of the Constitution. For Cubans this statement is clear, and we have availed ourselves of it accordingly.

Outside Cuba, however, this has bred two kinds of concerns. Some see it as being a kind of terrifying Sword of Damocles, sharpened so that the State might use it to crush whatever it decides to label as "counterrevolutionary." In actuality it has been otherwise: the slogan has worked out splendidly as a shield to defend ourselves against bureaucrats, dogmatists and other enemies of culture. It has even allowed us to attack them successfully, because cultural practice in Cuba is not monolithic, nor does it consist

Plastic Arts in Cuba

of a line "handed down from above." It is a struggle with triumphs and misfortunes of which I bear scars of my own, but, also, I have notches on my gun.

From an opposite extreme, others have considered this openness in Cuban culture to be a bourgeois-liberal weakness. Leaving art to the personal will of artists is taken as a concession grounded in the Romantic concept of the artist as a creative genius, detached from society. We have quite an issue here, even though the absolutist terms of this position make it essentially willful. Art, as we know it, is a very specialized activity, extremely dependent on individual subjectivity. If someone can only paint intimate flowers it would backfire to try to force him/her to make propaganda, even if she/he were painting political flowers. They would be bad flowers and bad politics. If intimate flowers elicit poetry in someone, this will be his/her social function, to paint them. The problem underlying much political art is that it ends up being weak art because it is an undertaking, rather than a natural offshoot of the living fabric of specificities and experiences of individual artists, imposed more from outside rather than coming from the inside. Besides, an art of direct social commission in a socialist country always runs the risk of lapsing into opportunism and bureaucratization.

Which is not to say that social undertakings, as such, are not valid. It would be another matter to seek a gradual transformation of the social role of art, with no traumas. It's not a question of whether artists should "descend" or "ascend" to the people, if they are at all capable of it; or, as a Spanish poet used to say, "to write for the people, what more could I wish for!" Nor is it a question of trying to make popular or populist art, or of increasing the number of those capable of understanding art through education, which would in fact boil down to a broadening or "socialization" of the elite. I am referring to a revolution in the whole system of the production, distribution and consumption of art, a system that has undergone almost no change in any socialist country. As to its structure, it works just the same with galleries, museums, publications and critics in Sofia, Boston or Havana, although with different goals and contents. The worst part is that a general awareness of the problem does not exist.

Facts are hard-headed, and a troublesome doubt lingers: is this only a utopian vision of the Russian productivists and of the radical thought of the Sixties? There is always the danger of unreality in understanding revolution as an all-encompassing transformation of everything, a sort of total leap into the future, and not as only the precipitous moment of an ongoing process of evolution. Socialism does not imply the formal negation of former structures, when they are still capable of serving new goals. This is clear from Soviet experience. Besides, socialism is not outside of history, nor is it devoid of context.

We must also take into account that what is presently called art is the result of a long process of specialization which, by the Romantic era, became defined as an autonomous activity. If the tendency is toward specialization, then art can only continue defining itself as a production of highly complex messages for specialists only, leaving so-called mass culture to take care of the rest. My stance is to struggle, without being naive, for a social transformation of art. If we do not attempt to put this into practice directly and indirectly, intermediately and immediately, then we will never know whether it is at all possible.

The cultural policy and practice of the Cuban Revolution may be roughly divided into three periods. The first, which we might call the romantic stage, went from liberation in 1959 until approximately 1970. Culture blossomed in an extraordinary fashion; a revolution took place in the moral and material support for culture. Institutions, schools and artistic groups were created, and the social role of the artist was enhanced. Cultural life thrived in an atmosphere of enthusiasm and freedom. This rare combination of state support and independence from state control was maintained during the "hard years," when the Revolution struggled for survival. Cuba, at that time, was in revolutionary and cultural ferment.

The second stage, which might be described as the dark period, put the brakes on this romantic upsurge. It lasted approximately from 1970 until 1982, and was bound up with the lost illusions of the Sixties and with the process of institutionalization in our country. This was a moment when the "stagnation period" of the Soviet Union exerted its influence on us. Cultural freedom was maintained and neither an official line nor socialist realism was imposed, but under the watchword "Art, a weapon of the revolution," politics and art were mixed together clumsily. An overly simplified interpretation of art's ideological role prevailed, and propaganda as well as superficial expressions of an almost stereotypical cultural identity were stimulated. Many of our best artists were not promoted, or worse, were pushed to the sidelines, while complacent mediocrity was fostered. It was an unfortunate period in which the essence of the political cultural policy of the Revolution was being contradicted.

In 1982 things began to change, with the opening of a period I would dare to call a kind of "renaissance." The creation of the Ministry of Culture, under Armando Hart[5], developed quite a coherent policy and reestablished a creative atmosphere that led to the upsurge in the 1980s of a new "unsoiled" generation, full of vitality. It was the visual arts that set the tone for this period.

This generation brought on change by going against former policies. Presently, it is the visual arts which make up the most forceful component of Cuban culture. In all of this I came to play a modest role; I happen to be the critic who wrote about the artists who brought about these changes, and I have been called that generation's ideologue. My ideas were expressed in the modest catalogs of the exhibits by young artists, in open discussions and, with greater difficulty, in magazines and books. This was criticism through participation, born in direct contact with the artists and seeking common viewpoints.

Our platform was quite simple. We wanted to encompass new avenues and resources that had sprung up in the visual arts since the end of the Sixties, particularly conceptual art, which was unknown in Cuba. We wanted art to defend its pursuits and artistic values, and not simply follow the watchwords of the moment and the convenience of public officals. (There were cases like when a Cuban cow broke the world record for milk production and, as an opportunistic reaction, referential art works sprung up and, in all seriousness, were extolled by a critic in an article titled "Art and Raising Cattle." When the cow died, a bronze monument was erected in its honor.) We also wanted to break with the dogma of national identity, which had also risen to ridiculous extremes. For instance, someone painted masks into pictures in order to express the African element, guitars for the Spanish touch, rupestrine drawings of the aborigines who were exterminated by the

17th century, palm trees to express the geography, rifles to connote the Revolution and bouncing buttocks for Caribbean sensuality.

The exhibition *"Volumen 1,"*[6] held in January 1981, was a great success and represented a milestone of the new changes. All the issues raised were addressed, thus bringing this dark period to a close. From then on, an endless number of pursuits developed in a polemical and enthusiastic environment. This prompted an outpouring of new, restless young visual artists. A far-reaching movement of renovation was unleashed. This was an extraordinarily encouraging moment, unique in the history of socialism, in which questions of great interest regarding art within a revolution were put forth. In what follows, I will sketch some of the general trends in this work.

ETHICS

The visual arts in Cuba have an ethical substratum in the deepest meaning of the word. There is a thoughtfulness about individual and social behavior and about the problems of human beings unfolding in a world which is becoming less and less straightforward. We could also speak of an anthropological concern. The basis and focus of such art are always ethical even when political questions are being discussed. Socialism is confronted as a moral value, as a possibility for full human realization, from a meditative and philosophical viewpoint, avoiding any kind of rhetoric. This concern anticipated the call to revolutionary consciousness which typifies the rectification process now going on in Cuba.[7]

IDENTITY

Paradoxically, cultural identity has again come to the fore, but in a diametrically opposed way. Cultural roots are not displayed—they are put to work. Identity becomes action from deep within oneself, and not an identity card. A deepening Latin Americanist spirit is forming, which is very significant for art in a country that for a long time ignored its continent to a large degree. There is also a deepening search into the Afro-Cuban elements of our culture. In both cases interest is focused on cosmic vision, on values and on mysticism, not on morphologies, rituals or mythological anecdotes. Artists often work from within, either because they are believers in Afro-Cuban religions or because they have grown up in environments where such religions predominate.

A Latin American, Third World and at the same time contemporaneous outlook is sought, capable of navigating in today's world. This has been of great interest to me, because it gives a glimmer of hope for solving the schisms in Third World cultural perspectives—between tradition and contemporaneity, independence and cultural colonialization, identity and mimesis, "primitivism" and post-modernism. Western culture (pertaining to a European tradition corresponding to the planetary expansion of industrial capitalism) has been imposed on the majority by a minority. This expansion is a feat of hegemonic power; it is inevitable, given the nature of contemporary life. For the Third World, the answer does not lie in copying, adapting or even "nationalizing" Western culture—these would be transitory solutions—nor in hiding one's head under precapitalist traditions. The solution for us is to make "Western" culture our own way and according to our own values and interests. When this happens, the terms "Western" and "contemporary" will cease to be synonymous and there will be a truly universal culture.

POPULAR CULTURE

Cuba is the only underdeveloped country with a system of art instruction providing free training for all talented children and young people. Thus, many artists come from the more humble strata of the population, of which they are still a part. We are seeing a certain phenomenon become generalized; these young people are the bearers of a popular culture and at the same time they are "cultured" artists. Even though their works are conceived in order to be shown in galleries, we find in them a natural, innermost, undistanced presence of the popular within the "cultured," a strange paradox that might tell us something about a future development of art arising from Third World countries—"cultured" manifestations of the "popular." Some time ago I said that formerly the "artist" used to paint "peasants," "blacks" and "workers;" whereas nowadays, the "peasant," "blacks" and "workers" have begun to be the "artists."

CRITICAL SENSE

A tendency toward social critique, having as its starting point the ethical stand mentioned above, is typical of the youngest artists working today in Cuba. Theirs is a strong, principled criticism, using satire in order to provoke thought rather than as a means of attack. Even if it begins with a specific denunciation, the goal of this work is to use the power of art to make us reflect on deeper problems underlying what is being denounced. For instance, one painter made a whole series of works about slogans which were, more than a jibe against sloganeering, a meditation on the problem of building socialism.

Criticism voiced through the visual arts echoes a popular restlessness that is only now becoming formalized. The visual arts have thus become the most daring forum in Cuba, and some performance pieces have turned into street demonstrations. In all the cases I know of, the issues were raised in a constructive manner, within and for the Revolution. They represent one more aspect of the critical moment that socialism is living through on a worldwide scale, in which a struggle is being waged against its internal enemies. These critical expressions were stimulated by issues recently raised by Fidel Castro himself, who insisted that freedom of creativity includes content as well as form, and that the *raison d'être* of socialism is raising that freedom to the highest degree. This theory, together with what is actually happening, opens up new challenges for the relationship between art and politics under socialism.

SOCIAL CONCERN

The younger artists are strongly driven to revolutionize the social role of the visual arts. In general, their work takes the form of actions, manifestos and works in alternative spaces, such as the recent project placing serigraphs in city buses, most of which dealt with the microcosm of the famous Havana *guaguas* (buses), and which appealed directly to the passengers. Even in conventional gallery work there is a notable lack of concern for the individual "aura" of a work of art, which is gladly sacrificed in order to address socially relevant issues.

The most radical minds want to break up the whole production-consumption system and the mentality which goes along with it (which I outlined previously), and pursue a true socialization of art. They are aware of the difficulties involved, starting with their own educational background, which prepared them to act as "individual geniuses" within the system. They regard the whole business as a long process that includes a "healing" of the artists themselves. Toward this end an experiment is now going on in the rural community of Pilón, conducted by a group of young artists working with the support of the Ministry of Culture. Their purpose is to design a systematic plan of cultural development for this underserved community. The work must cut across the social scale—it must not be for the elite—in order to break out of conformity. Perhaps all these projects may bring us face to face with the most important cultural initiative in the history of the visual arts of the Revolution, precisely because it might be the only wholly revolutionary approach that has been undertaken. My own stance is to back it wholeheartedly, even though I remain a pessimist about its eventual success. Anyway this active utopianism is worth it, even if only for the sake of raising an awareness of the contradictions between art and society that persist under socialism.

The points I have outlined dovetail into each other and are the key to the unique movement taking place in Cuban visual arts. It is making Cuban culture live through one of its most invigorating moments. My greatest satisfaction lies in having contributed to its arising, and in continuing to play an active role within it.

Translated by Alan West.

THE ENIGMA OF CHILE

TRANSCRIPT OF REMARKS

BY CECILIA VICUÑA[1]

The shamanic tradition in Chile is very much alive; there are a million Mapuche people who continue to practice their old religion, in spite of 500 years of intervention. Now, what's happening is that there is so much cultural segregation in Chile that most people have no idea of the shamanic tradition. The Mapuche oral poetical tradition has been completely wiped out, and very few intellectuals know it or study it. Neruda, for example, who grew up in the middle of Mapuche territory in the south of Chile, gave as testimony of that segregation the fact that in his childhood he saw the Mapuches pass by like distant shadows; he never had any contact with them. And it's not that he was unusual in this regard, but simply because Chileans of different classes and races did not mix among themselves, and mixed even less with the Mapuches.

Now, in the time of the dictatorship, people often say that Chile is a divided country, that Pinochet has created a civilization of science fiction. They say that it is like Copenhagen and Calcutta at the same time; that from the middle to the top it's perfect, impeccable, there is not one scrap of paper on the ground. And from the middle down, it is a total disaster. But curiously enough the metaphors that Chileans use to speak of this situation describe

Transcript of Remarks

the two Chiles as a country that is European and African; it is curious, because there is practically no population of African origin in Chile, so this is a way of avoiding saying "European and Indian." That is how they have erased everything indigenous.

It is interesting to see in this duality the fact that whenever there is a dark part, it is the part that contains the metamorphosis. There the darkened side is not only the indigenous culture, it is the women who sing. The wisdom is nourished by the women. The *machi* is the woman-shaman and this tradition remains absolutely alive. She is the woman who cures with her chant, and she is the one who establishes the unity of the community.

I would like to relate what I am saying to the triumph of the NO vote in Chile. For me, from a metaphorical point of view, the triumph of the NO has transformed a negation into an affirmation. For me, Chile has lived denying its own being for 500 years, denying our racial mixture, denying the fact that we are two things in one. I am going to come back to the subject of the NO, but first I want to talk about the matter of racial mixture.

At this moment, if one uses the word "*mestizo*" (mixed blood, cross-breed), one comes up against two meanings. For the Indians, a "*mestizo*" is a traitor and an exploiter. For a white, on the other hand, a "*mestizo*" is an inferior person. From a poetical point of view, if one speaks of mestiza poetry, it is understood that one is speaking of poetry from the colonial period, that is, impure in relation to the oral tradition.

I call these words the "wounded" words, because there are various key words that nobody wants to use at this moment, but that represent precisely the essence of what we must cure or transform. This connects up with the millenia-old tradition that exists in South America of talking backwards. For example if it's very hot in Chile, people say "it is cold!" If somebody is despicable, people say he is a fabulous guy. It is, in fact, a habit that everybody practices. Now, nobody knows that this is a pre-Columbian custom; Chile is also a country with a strong Andalusian influx and the Andalusians, who are gypsies, also like to talk backwards.

In any case, I would like to speak of the pre-Columbian tradition. In ancient times, to know how to play with words was counted as wisdom, because words were sacred. Breath was borrowed from a divinity, breath was an entity that did not belong to the individual. So then if words are sacred, they have power, and it is natural that breath is sacred because the earth is sacred, air is sacred, water is sacred. So then to play with words was to understand the forces that moved the words. Therefore, the one who knew how to play with words was a sage. The words were kinetic energy, and to participate in that energy was to affect it. The people in Chile nowadays play a great deal with words, they turn them over all the time. The tradition is still alive.

Returning to Pinochet. When he forced us to accept the plebiscite, everybody said he didn't know what he was getting into. Because curiously enough what he was doing was to set free the power of people to talk. During all those years of dictatorship he had abused the language, he had imposed terror and lies. In Spanish, the word *"mentiras"* (lies) divides into "men[te]" (mind) and "tira" (tear); *"mentira"* means "lies tear apart the mind." Then, when the people took the NO and turned the negation of life into an affirmation of life, they were using this same tradition of playing with words to their advantage. They erased the lie in order to establish the truth; truth, *"verdad"* in Spanish, means to "dar ver," to "give sight."

QUESTIONS FROM THE AUDIENCE

Question about the relationship of both the democratic and dictatorial governments to the indigenous population.

CV: A good question. During the Popular Front government, the only good laws that have ever existed in Chile for the indigenous community were enacted and put into force; indigenous rights were protected for the first time. Directives were issued, in their own language, giving them the right to keep and maintain their communal lands, and many other things. But when the dictatorship was barely in power, all those laws were revoked, and the laws imposed by the dictatorship are the worst that have ever been passed as far as the Mapuche community is concerned. For example Pinochet's laws even erase the word "Mapuche" from the wording of the legislation; they are now called *"campesinos,"* or

Transcript of Remarks

farm workers.

So then, the ancestral lands they have managed to save, in spite of all these years, can now be sold if only one person in the community demands that they be sold. The Mapuche community has managed to preserve their language, their vision of the world, their customs, their thought—a thought of great metaphorical and metaphysical richness—and have also managed to maintain all their ethno-botanical knowledge and, thanks to that, they have preserved their land. So then, if they lose the land, their culture will disintegrate; that was, obviously, the political intention of the dictatorship.

Now, in recent years, there has been a movement among young people to take an interest in these matters. Until a short while ago, I thought that I was one of the few poets to be concerned with the Mapuche culture and its preservation, but now I have discovered another poet, Juan Pablo Rivero, from Concepción in the south, a man about my own age, who has written an extraordinary book called *La tierra sin fuego (The Land Without Fire,* a play on the name of "Tierra del Fuego," "Land of Fire"). The book is dedicated to the Fuegian people. There are also some others who are beginning to work with indigenous themes, so one sees, bit by bit, a kind of discovery of that erased culture. All this will change in the future, obviously; I believe that when a democratic government comes, there will be many people pressuring the government for laws that will protect the Mapuches.

Translated by Cola Franzen.

MARJORIE AGOSIN

To talk about what one writes, or to write about what one says nowadays turns into a strange paradox. How to write about what is so often forbidden to say? How to speak about what is kept silent? How to invent strategies to unmask deaths, tortures, burnings?

The act of writing now becomes an ethical stance, the ethic of denunciation, the ethic that says no to silence. So my writing is linked to the speech of those who do not speak.

Gags, blindfolds, mute women, women of smoke make up my texts, but my texts come also from the stratum of the imagination, from invented nostalgia, articulated through words in distant, prostrate lands.

Distanced from Chile, I started to use the same distance to begin a dialogue with the poisoned country; I came to understand that the only possible place to live is in the country that we invent day by day.

Blindfolded but alive, I recreate landscapes: the undaunted silent Cordillera immersed in the colors of blood. Rippling seas peopled by shipwrecked bodies. Peaches and sun. My poetry is nourished by fruits eaten years ago during a childhood that beckons me and becomes more substantial as words are traced out.

I invent countries and I invent myself, but I go back to the stories of the country, stories of forgotten women and wanderers. I think about these women and I write about them because I am one of them. *Witches and Other Things*[1] reflects my preoccupation with women who take chances, with those who risk being burned in bonfires. In this book the Witch of the title is not a synonym for evil but for the power and magic found in the body of a woman, a body that recreates and creates life.

Middle-class women, witches, prostitutes, odes to garlic, odes against the *machista* tradition of Chilean poetry appear in this first bilingual collection of mine. Seeing my work in translation makes me more like or brings me nearer to this life in a permanent state of invention in another language, lets me cross boundaries, brings me closer to the other. Because my poetry born in a distant country has to be that other.

After *Witches* I wrote another collection of poetry called *Bonfires*[2]. Unconsciously, one work grows out of another. But here bonfires do not deal with burning, but with bringing to life, reviving. *Bonfires* is a book dedicated to love, meant to celebrate love. I wanted to write it and have it published in Chile as a gesture of survival, as homage to those suffering, to paraplegics, to those who can't sleep. It seemed to me that one way of not letting the dictatorship win was to write a book of love poems.

The poems in *Bonfires* are about women initiating and enjoying love rather than simply receiving love from a man. She is the one who takes her pleasure, the enchantress, who instructs him and says:

> If patiently
> you touch my
> thighs,
> you'll find
> the light of leaves
> the dreams of chloroform
>
> If you come down
> into the moistened
> shiver

of my lips
you'll find
God
winking at you.[3]

Bonfires brings me close to the fulfillment of the inexplicable and above all to the mirror of the body, because the body is a celebratory act.

Everything turns into
festival
when you take my clothes off
and
I perfume
the mouths
of love.

Perhaps my obsession for the body lies in the obsession for the tortured body. In *Bonfires* I suggest that the body exists only when it is recognized by the other. I wanted to deny pain, that pain inflicted deliberately and knowingly, the kind of pain that only the tortured experiences while the torturer looks on and watches. *Bonfires* is the opposite, it is a song of celebration that says: here I am, come with me across rivers and seas:

We could have been a
single river
a single arm of water

Women of Smoke[4], conceived and written after *Bonfires,* is not in response to a lack of love but creates a space inhabited by sick women—sick according to the ideas of others. I was preoccupied with the ambience of mad and feverish housewives cleaning their brocade sofas. I wanted to speak of the woman who celebrates the witch's sabbath of solitude, whose vigil illuminates the night so that later her house and the celebration of her own death may be illuminated. In *Women of Smoke* I approach the shadowy world of vagabond women, madwomen, those who take to drink, unfaithful women in shabby motel rooms. With *Women of Smoke*

Marjorie Agosín

I enter the dark rooms of lonely women and I wrote this collection in the form of delirium, as another gesture or act of love for women who have nothing, not even a voice.

> Unbalanced
> she bespoke fresh words to come
> she kept them separated from those
> already said.
> She was a flying acrobat of languages
> because she asked to speak
> amid a
> hollow silence.

After *Women of Smoke* I wrote *Zones of Pain*[5]. The nostalgia—or musing aloud—about the country takes on more and more of a precise reality: torture, the massacred body is no longer imagined and real people emerge so they will not be forgotten. *Zones of Pain* is the story of the women who disappeared, who began to inhabit my dreams like the dreams of others.

> Slowly and in secret
> the roof of my silenced mouth burning
> and I already naked and
> so far away
> conspiring to trap
> my nipples, thin wires of terror.
> Their small fingers, sloughed off scales of bitter wormwood
> venture along that slow agony, through obscured brightness between my legs.
>
> ("Torture," from *las zonas del dolor/Zones of Pain*)

The women began to awaken within me, and during the vigil, I saw them with flowers in their hair going in search of tombs for their burials. They call out so that they may be found because they exist only when we search for them or discover them.

I had no witnesses
to my death.
Nobody carried out rituals, wrote epitaphs.
Nobody came near
for a veiled
farewell.

To call the names of the disappeared women implies bringing the mutilated bodies back to life and gives rise to so many questions. How does a disappeared woman see the light? How does a blindfolded woman experience light, vision, breezes? What question lies behind the searching?

Beyond the dawn
clothed in fog,
they ask her
why are you weeping?
whom are you seeking?
—she only said to them
give me back my
daughter.

More than an encounter with writing, *Zones of Pain* represents for me an encounter with myself and with the authenticity of what I write. One must speak of pain without euphemisms, just as one must speak of the *picanas,* the electric prods used in torture, prowling over the skin of the helpless.

Zones of Pain is a brutal confrontation with the martyred country, a country no longer a wraith of smoke and fog. It is a country that howls, but the scream is ear-splitting silence.

After *Zones of Pain,* or more accurately almost at the same time, I began to make the poetical experience more concrete, so that the words would not be simply a closed relationship between reader and writer.

Scraps of Life[6] is another fundamental form of my writing and ties together everything said earlier. It describes my personal experiences with a group of Chilean women from the shantytowns of Santiago, scourged by hunger, misery and the disappearance of their loved ones. In order to appease hunger as well as to heal the deep wounds caused by their disappeared, they began to make small wall hangings called *arpilleras,* using left-over scraps of cloth. The *arpilleras* recreate all the despair as well as the pleasures of their daily life, an immense sun above the Cordillera of the Andes illuminating them.

For me the *arpilleras* are one of the truest forms of writing; writing done by women with needle and thread. In that way they tell their stories by means of visual images since the right to speak is denied them.

Out of my experiences with them came what I consider my most important work so far: to write about them, help them to tell that story so that it will be known and not blown away by the wind. Writing about their lives, describing their tapestries, constitutes an essential part of the history of Chile within the heart of the country. To see those anonymous tapestries winging their way around the world gives a clear message: the women embroider their lives, their bodies, so as not to forget, so as not to be silenced.

José Daniel, the collection of poems I am working on now, is the story of my son with his hands like flour, incredulous, innocent, newly-born. I am writing for him, and as I sing to him I immerse myself once again in the engima that is Chile. Again I seem to sleepwalk and float through emerald lakes and seas; the obsessive Cordillera waits for us, but I also invent a country for my son:

> I invented you a
> country
> in bedtime stories
> and in a language from the farthest corner
> of a foreign place
> I speak to you of Chile lying to you
> by not mentioning
> massacred bodies
> you ask me for bedtime stories
> and I sing to you
> Jose Daniel
> invent for you
> enchanted

cities
countries of smoke.

And even if they keep me blindfolded always, I will always find my way back to Chile.

QUESTIONS FROM THE AUDIENCE

Question about what Agosín will write once Pinochet is removed from power.

M.A.: First I plan to write more about joy and enjoy life more. And second, I think it is terribly important not to forget the dead. And I believe that we should continue with that preoccupation of speaking of them, because if we do not remember them, their deaths will really have been in vain. I believe there are two things we will need: a new kind of optimism, and at the same time a determination not to forget the disappeared. That is the attitude expressed by the Mothers of the Plaza de Mayo and by women in other similar movements.

Question about *machismo,* and about women's rights in Chile.

M.A.: Yes, I believe that *machismo* exists in Chile, that it is still being practiced, and that it is most visible in the field of literature where women continue to be pushed to the sidelines. Above all, for a woman to publish in Chile is truly a daring act, a sacrifice, and the same thing holds true for some men too, but I believe that men have kowtowed much more to the power structure and to the big daily newspapers; even many poets of the left have been willing to compromise in order to get published in right wing newspapers such as the *Mercurio* in Santiago. And not many women have played that game, and for that reason also they have been kept on the sidelines. I believe that the Chilean literary movement, particularly during these last 15 years, has remained very much dominated by men. But fortunately women finally decided that they were going to write for themselves and organize their own readings, their own anthologies, and I believe that that initial effort by women brought about a change. But I continue to think that the writer in Chile is terribly *machista*.

Translated by Cola Franzen.

CULTURE AND INDEPENDENCE
IN PUERTO RICO

CULTURE AND INDEPENDENCE IN PUERTO RICO

MARTIN ESPADA

We Live by What We See at Night
—for my father

When the mountains of Puerto Rico
flickered in your sleep
with a moist green light,
when you saw green bamboo hillsides
before waking to East Harlem rooftops
or Texas barracks,
when you crossed the bridge
built by your grandfather
over a river glimpsed
only in interrupted dreaming,
your craving for that island birthplace
burrowed, deep
as thirty years' exile,
constant as your pulse.

Culture and Independence in Puerto Rico

This was the inheritance
of your son, born in New York:
that years before
I saw Puerto Rico,
I saw the mountains
looming above the projects,
overwhelming Brooklyn,
living by what I saw at night,
with my eyes closed.

This is the connection between Puerto Rico and Puerto Ricans in the United States. We survive here because of the strength we have gathered from that island. And yet, we are only here because Puerto Rico is a colony of the United States, and as such has failed us, so much so that from the late 1940s through the mid-1960s fully one third of the population left the island, looking for work, looking for another life.

Puerto Rico is a colony. Any country which is the territory of another country is a colony. Any country taken as a prize of war, as Puerto Rico was in the Spanish-American War of 1898, is a colony. Any country where the young men can be drafted to fight in the wars of another country is a colony. Any country which has no control over its foreign policy, trade policy, military, immigration laws, environmental laws, minimum wage, tariffs and duties, currency or appeals courts is a colony. Characteristic of a colony, Puerto Rico is both economically exploited and economically dependent; and those who have advocated real change, that is, independence, have been discriminated against, repressed, jailed and sometimes killed. Colonialism is inherently wrong, even as practiced by the United States with all its rhetoric of good intentions, beginning with General Nelson Miles when he invaded our island in 1898 bringing, as he put it, "the blessings of our enlightened civilization."

A colony has an official history, of the kind found in textbooks and tourist brochures, which leaves out the rest. The artist in the colonial context must remember "the rest." The artist must serve as the popular memory, the popular voice, dissenting from the official history. He or she must be, in the words of one such writer, Clemente Soto Vélez, as translated:

blood
that
keeps
singing
after it congeals
to circulate
radiating through the insurrection
of its arteries

By remembering insurrection, we can reawaken the potential for insurrection in ourselves, can see clearly again the need for insurrection.

In the 1930s, there was a major political movement for independence, with the rise of the Nationalist Party. Its leaders were imprisoned for sedition in 1936. When their followers protested in Ponce on Palm Sunday, 1937, police killed 21 and wounded over 150 in an incident known as the Ponce Massacre. Historical memory: recently, a friend told me about his mother and her husband-to-be, and how their lives were caught up in the Ponce Massacre. This poem resulted:

Rebellion is the Circle of a Lover's Hands:
Pellín and Nina

The marchers gathered, Nationalists
massed beneath the delicate white balconies
of Marina Street,
and the colonial governor
pronounced the order with patrician calm:
fifty years of family history
says it was Pellín
who dipped a finger
into the bloody soup of his own body
and scratched defiance
in jagged wet letters on the sidewalk.
Around him stormed
the frenzied clattering drumbeat
of machineguns,
the stampede of terrified limbs

and the panicked wail
that rushed babbling
past his dim senses.

Palm Sunday, 1937:
the news
halted the circular motion
of his lover's hands
as she embroidered
the wedding dress.
She nodded, knew
before she was told.

Years later, with another family
in a country of freezing spring rain
called Nueva York,
Nina is quietly nervous
when her son speaks of rifles
in a bullhorn shout,
when coffins are again bobbing
on the furious swell of hands and shoulders,
and the whip of nightsticks
brings fresh blood
stinging from the scalp.

But rebellion
is the circle of a lover's hands,
that must keep moving,
always weaving.

    The nexus between art and politics in Puerto Rico is strong. Three of the Nationalist leaders imprisoned in 1936 were poets. One, Juan Antonio Corretjer, later became the national poet of Puerto Rico. Despite this distinction, Corretjer served a total of 12 years in prison over his lifetime, and was hounded by authorities till his death at the age of 76.
    Another of those poets, Clemente Soto Vélez, served a total of seven years in prison at various times. He is now 83 years old. I once asked what evidence was used against him at the 1936 trials.

Martín Espada

His answer formed the basis of this poem:

Clemente's Bullets

Half a century ago,
when the island was stripped of cane
and machetes slashed instead
at the soldiers of empire,
Clemente was a poet in a bow tie
with a gaze
like the mirror of heat on black water,
and the storm-crackle
of his voice
swept the crowds chanting
into the plaza's brilliant noon.
From the podium,
his hands beat the air
like the wings of leashed birds,
orchestrating the heart-rhythm of fists,
the strikers' song.
His words became
the prosecutor's evidence:
"Puerto Rican,
the independence of Puerto Rico
depends on the number of bullets
in your belt."

Sedition, said the general's jury:
six years in prison,
ceilings and floors
huge and gray
as the sides of a battleship
occupying the harbor of his sleep,
smuggling poems
fragment by fragment, words like
wooden horses and cows of stone,
during searched and scrutinized visits.
The years' damp
warped the joints of his fingers,

and Clemente learned to breathe
through the clogged lungs
of rasping solitary days.

Since then,
an island of plundered graves and gardens
has drained refugees from the mud,
clay-dark laborers migrating north.
In New York, his long white hair
is winter sky, the smoke of cities
taken by the rebels at last,
as Clemente remembers the language of bullets,
the prosecutor's evidence
that looted his lungs
and abducted the grace of his fingers.

Now when Clemente shouts a poem
his brittle hands are holy,
veined with the lightning of prophecy,
when revolution will race
across the plaza
with a barking of rifles,
and he will awaken
to a morning
in 1936.

It is a sad and significant commentary when a nation imprisons its poets. Corretjer and Soto Vélez were imprisoned; not by coincidence, the work of these two major writers is almost completely unavailable in the United States, in Spanish or in translation. But, to use his own words, as translated, Clemente Soto Vélez:

> may as well have been born
> wherever freedom
> grows like children

His words cannot be jailed like the man. Repression is never that easy.

As Puerto Rican artists, our search for independence becomes a search into our communities and into ourselves: a search for a national identity, a cultural identity, a racial identity, a personal identity, and they are all linked. We must, and often do, accept our responsibility to create in our people the self-confidence necessary for self-defense, awakening the realization that with national and individual independence comes freedom from contempt. We must see to it that, for every [Boston radio station] WBCN reporter who says that her hotel at the Democratic convention in Atlanta was so bad "even the Puerto Ricans have left," there is a poem or painting or a song that reminds us of our human dignity and our legacy of resistance, all 500 years' worth. I will close with a poem which epitomizes my own search. The title, "Cordillera," refers to a mountain chain in Puerto Rico, but refers also to a chain of history and culture and family and struggle over centuries:

Cordillera

Far from beggars' hands
searching in cities
of Iberian cobblestone,
the mountains rest,
a council of elders
drowsing in the market square.

The rain forests are steaming
and sluggish, green palm
and broken rock
proud and broad
like the cheekbones
of an extinct people.

Older than suffering:

the mountains are shaman,
guarding the caves
from archaeologists;
the mountains are guerrilleros,
rising together

to swallow terrified armies;
the mountains are peasants,
great shoulders breaking the earth
to spring forth crops.

Lares, Jayuya, Utuado,
towns of the mountain
where rebellion's song wept
like slaves in the joy
of abolition,
rang like a machete forged
by insurgent blacksmiths,
raged like a rainstorm
deep in the chest of mountains.

We are of mountains.

Descended from Taíno carvings,
Spanish watchtowers,
African manacles,
the jíbaro plow,

the only glimpse
a Victorian photograph
of minor officials,
shirtsleeved and tough;
a brick from the house
where my father was born.

I will disappear
in Borinquén's mountains,
lost among boulders,
drinking from
mottled creekbeds,
exploring unknown gardens,
discovering hungry shacks
and wild sow
in green plantain thicket,
searching like those

beggars' hands
for bread and sight
and salvation.

JUAN SANCHEZ

The artist, like the writer, has the obligation to be of use;
his painting must be a book that teaches;
it must serve to better the human condition;
it must castigate evil and exalt virtue.
—Francisco Oller (1833-1917)

Colonialism is an epidemic—a widespread, evil contagion, like a disease; an uncontrollable, prevailing condition. The damage it causes is physical, mental and even metaphysical. It is a crushing colonial mindset that dominates Puerto Rican land and culture, and its end result is worse than an earthquake. This imperialist epidemic constantly confuses—free, associated state?—to keep our focus diverted from the source of our national problem, to pretend it does not exist. We can see the epidemic advancing, for instance, in the sterilization of more than a third of all Puerto Rican women of child-bearing age by a United States-sponsored program meant to "control overpopulation and unemployment"—one of the highest rates of genocidal sterilization in the world. We have seen death advancing before our eyes, like fighters in the longest of battles. Sometimes it is a hidden epi-

Juan Sanchez
"A Puerto Rican Prisoner of War and Much More"
1983
Oil, acrylic, mixed media on canvas, 78" x 54"

Juan Sanchez
"La Lucha Continua"
1986
Mixed media print, 22" x 30"

demic; sometimes it is nowhere to be seen and cannot be hit or even targeted. In this battle there are times when only the enemy is active, striking and eating where he chooses, striking down so many that a loss of perspective might lead us to the despair of finding a way out, of changing the situation. In a climate of despair, the epidemic produces a people of death and dying. Colonialism is a slow death.

My art is empirical, probing into the social and political basis of my Puerto Rican heritage and reality. My work deals with cultural definition, and with a search for roots. The combination of Taíno Indian petroglyphs from pre-Columbian Borinquén, the saints and *orishas* of popular African and Catholic religion, and the gritty ghetto environment of my birthplace, New York City, are what contribute to my identity. I express all of these in my paintings and prints. The rich visual and cultural language, through the painted and drawn image together with the photographic images and written texts, enable me to speak on a conscious as well as a subconscious level. In reality, I use visual language more to channel an outpouring of feelings and socio-political concerns which take on a more personal perspective, for the sake of creating an awareness of the political plight of the Puerto Rican people as they struggle for freedom and self-determination. I call upon racial memory, experience and dignity to give my art direction, as our struggle and search for destiny continue. Faith is fundamental in my creative expressions. Collective cultural forces express the love, joy, anger and even despair that erupts from the oppressive/repressive situations in which we are locked.

I try to imbue my creative expressions with the history of our struggle for liberation, which is deeply rooted in the r/evolution of culture as an aesthetic for truth and justice. My images also recall the momentous historical events of past generations; dismemberment of the colony, the migration of masses of our people as wage-laborers, and the growth and development of the new community in a radically different, hostile, racist economic/political/cultural setting on the U.S. mainland. I am very committed to the education of our people, to protecting our cultural integrity and roots, to reasserting the positive, progressive values of our heritage. By staying close to feelings, to universal truths, concerns, beliefs and needs, it is my sincere hope that my art, as well as

Juan Sánchez

the art, writing, theatre and music made by individuals like myself, will help pave the way for that glorious day when, suppression notwithstanding, we rid ourselves of this evil epidemic and as a people become a true nation, a free and sovereign people.

Juan Sanchez
"Un Sueno Libre"
1987
Lithography, Xerox, collage, 22" x 30"

BREGANDO[1]

LUIS RAFAEL SANCHEZ

The word *bregando* has two faces, like some people; two faces that are surely more charming than they are pretty. With one, it looks at the slums; with the other, the homes of the wealthy. You will have noticed that in both visages there is a kind of cheerful ugliness, so purely Puerto Rican. Should it smile, the ugliness does not offend whereas, if it is haughty, beauty offends.

But are there only two faces to the word *bregando?* No. There are two destinies which tempt it, the slum and the posh estate. And there are two generalizations which underlie the use of *bregando* by the Papo Swing[2] of the moment, who speaks in alternate registers—lumpen or super-refined—and who always makes things worse. Later, the two destinies hook up with others that are less easy to stereotype. Later, the two destinies multiply more rapidly than orangutans through the rear-view mirrors of St. Christopher. And later, at last, the use to the point of abuse of *bregando,* turns it into a word that is *fresh, sassy, meddlesome, cheeky, brazen,* according to the different kinds of recrimination applied by popular wisdom, that wisdom that hasn't yet graduated.

A voyage toward *bregando*'s multiplicities isn't harmful. On the

Bregando

contrary, it helps appreciate the word's functions: as cushion or umbrella, as aspirin or pass-key. Above all, to hear it go in and out of itself with semantic cunning. How varied are the functions of *bregando*. But, not so many, at least not as many as the ideas it puts into motion, the keys of the Puerto Rican self, a keyboard which is activated with or without wanting to, revealing the expressive shortcuts with which you have to *bregar.*

It is a gerund with the tentacles of an octopus, a gerund enjoyed by polysemy, a memorable verb which in its abstraction is like a memorable abstract painting by Luis Hernandez Cruz or Fernando de Szyszlo, of an adverbial nature, if you *bregar* with mode or condition. The word *bregando* is legitimized by the dictionary by means of a father in the infinitive, which heads towards two mountain peaks: a Gothic one, with *brikan,* and Latin is the other, with *plicare.*

Linguistic mountains swallow things up like jungles: they swallow, devour and assimilate. But, eventually, they converge, mix together and even exchange voices, or lend them to each other. Don't we say the word *kindergarten* with the greatest of ease, as if we were Teutonic? Aren't we showing an aversion to using the equivalent in Spanish, our childhood garden, which seems mannered to us? It's a wispy example but, just the same, weighty. At times, languages are the least dogmatic respites of history. At times, the history of a language presents itself as a sensible alternative to a "history" of history.

History aside, let us *bregar,* immediately, with language. Or more aptly put, with the terms *brikan* and *plicare* without forgetting that Gothic is the Germanic language spoken by the Goths, and Latin the language of Latium spoken by the ancient Romans. By the way, it was *bregando* with the profitable mysteries of a bewitching language, a spell to the ear and an ability to unhinge the faculties of reason, that the Catholic Church built its millenary empire; by *bregando* with divine words in Latin that the faithful didn't know, Latin words which the faithful feared.

Bregar, that is, *brikan,* means to strike a blow in Gothic. And to strike something brings into play similar ideas of struggle, quarrelling, tussling and wrangling with one another. It also means hustle and bustle, to wear oneself out, get upset, to work real hard at something. Figuratively, it also means to struggle with risks or tasks or difficulties in order to overcome them. *Bregar,* that is, *plicare,* means to fold, bend, bend over, and these words bring to mind a companion word, to knead. Enough for now with the *brega* of etymologies. Enough for now with the *brega* of meanings.

It's not without good reason that the greyhound sports a long tail. The *brega* of Puerto Ricans is a waggish and clever grafting onto of the above-mentioned meanings. Like a stew or an *asopao*[3] made of succulent and abundant sayings. And *bregando* is the clever and waggish sprouting of *bregar.* Like the little piece of ham that pulls along with it clumps of plantain, bits of squash and through which grains of rice appear, floating.

So by belaboring normative grammar we stumble on culinary grammar! So by extracting the juices of *bregando,* we rekindle the memory of home cooking and the *friquitín*[4], the nostalgia of the *alcapurria*[5] and the *pionono*[6], of the *jíbaro envuelto*[7] and the *yanicleca*[8], of the *almojábana*[9] from Humacao and the grease crackling in the pan. By transcribing the ingredients of *bregando,* we wind up with the most cherished pleasures, the versatile pleasures of the tongue: speaking and eating, eating and speaking, it doesn't matter in which order.

Is this a manifestation of the collective unconscious awakened by the fragrance of goat fricassee, or that of blood sausage? The remembrance of things enjoyed in *El imán de Cucú* by the thickets in Piñones, in *Nicolás y los demás*[10] by the palm trees in Luquillo, in the eatery called Librada in the neighboring areas of Monacillos, by the four little tables in back at Justo's tavern out there in Jájome? Some Freudian or Proustian is out there, somewhere, *bregando,* in order to answer the question and get his doctorate. With their Freudian and Proustian permission, I'd like to answer by asking the following.

Isn't it by *bregando* to eliminate the prosodic accent of the breadfruit and *mofongo*[11], that our language becomes a succulent creole dish that's kind of scary? Isn't it by *bregando* to remove the suspension points from a stuffed chayote that our language irreverently flouts all the norms of good academic manners? Isn't it by *bregando* to gobble up a pig's foot that we, uniquely, pronounce all the "s"'s that have ever existed? Isn't it by *bregando* with our tongue—with which we eat and speak at the same time—that we confirm the only possible bilingualism here? *Bregando* is humorous, for sure. *Bregando* tongue in cheek you talk away the unchanging bad times with which one has to deal (*bregando*). To be manipulative is *bregando*. So *bregando* with painful emotion you narrate the melodrama you're dealing with. And *bregando* is to behave more seriously than a founding father's armpit. And *bregando* relaxes you more than a parrot educated by whores. And *bregando* is one and plural, like everything here, or almost everything. Here in these bitter tropics that the great poetess sings to. Here, where the passing of the days makes one resentful and satisfied, and floods you with hope and desolation.

Do we need to repeat that "here" means Puerto Rico, the smallest of the Greater Antilles and the largest of the Lesser Antilles? Let there be no misunderstanding: this is not a tongue-twister, nor the apotheosis of an adverb of quantity, nor a case of erroneous syntax. The cute little geographic dissertation is injected into each little Puerto Rican child when they are *bregando* in elementary school, with the adroit caution needed to address the issue of the two flags, the two anthems and the sophism of homeland and nation: *Puerto Rico is the homeland, the U.S.A. is the nation.* Or how to be, furiously, exact. The insignificance of our little homeland has its own baby talk and nursing bottle, which lulls and stupefies, from infancy onwards.

Here everything is incriminated by the size of the country: vocation, sensibility, art, politics, even destiny. Here everything is transformed by the size of the country: mediocrity, cliques, cronyism, intellectual dispersion, and the familiarity that breeds contempt. *How can s/he be a major talent if s/he eats breakfast where I do?* Here everything is exhausted by the size of the country: equanimity, independence of criteria, the enjoyment of creative solitude, the denunciation of frivolous infighting. Here the exhaustion, the transparency, the incrimination spill over and wind up in the ocean of prejudice. Then, the baby talk and nursing bottle take on their effectiveness.

Because it puts blinders on the capacity for analysis, because accusations are wielded in order to discredit, the transparency and exhaustion produce a rancid and twisted fruit, created by the ugly Puerto Rican. He spends life *bregando* to soil his own nest, like a renegade bird. The ugly Puerto Rican who is not moved by any Puerto Rican conquest of the imagination, nor is he appreciative of any exploit of the Puerto Rican spirit. The ugly Puerto Rican thinks that any Puerto Rican landscape isn't sufficiently a landscape, that any Puerto Rican person isn't sufficiently a person. The ugly Puerto Rican who stubbornly disbelieves in the Puerto Rican capacity to organize a prosperous and open society, free of snooping and meddlesomeness. The ugly Puerto Rican to whom lucidity, careful thought, genius, are unscalable heights impossible to achieve here, in the smallest of the Greater Antilles and the biggest of the Lesser Antilles.

What else is *bregando?* So piercing that is, so French and so radical, so Cartesian, so like the impassioned Roland Barthes in his *A Lover's Discourse: Fragments.* Let's see how we're going to *bregar* with this answer. Let's see what kind of dialectical resources we can lay our hands on to dig up meanings of *bregando* yet to be seen and heard. Let's see what coasts of *bregando* we've yet to circle around. Let's see if four or five paragraphs are enough to finish this article with which I've been *bregando* for the last four or five days. An article, for sure, that Violante didn't ask me to do. It is an article that the "holy will" told me to do, influenced by the fits and starts of *bregando.* Is it a paradox to write about a will that can be influenced? Is it a matter of style and beauty? Is it an attempt to lead one astray, to be later rounded up by the *Irreal Academia de la Lengua*[12]? I don't know, and forgive me for my necklace of ignorances. Let the experts on style *bregar* with beauty, the philosopher with paradoxes and the academy with dispossessed words while I continue to *bregar* with *bregando.*

So *bregando* is another example of the adaptable nature of language, of its pleasing mien, which is its backbone. And of its capacity to be fashionable and traditional, of noticing the fleeting word and those that will endure. May the fields and the cemeteries argue over words, like dogs wrangling over bones. *Bregando* equally shows the compromise struck between language and crude orality; orality that literature likes to take on (*bregar*) by filtering through torturous fates, painful and crude fates. Can the transcriptions of Sancho Panza's spoken words—with which Cervantes had

Bregando

to *bregar*—ever be forgotten? Can the eradications made to the way the *gauchos* spoke—which *Martin Fierro* dealt with (*bregar*) ever be forgotten? Is there only one color missing in the *brega jibarista*[13] of Abelardo Diaz Alfaro?

Even so, every now and then, this idiomatic flexibility offends those who are stooped over, using the Covarrubias dictionary as a roof. Even so, every now and then the gendarmes of language levy a fine on that compromise between literature and orality. Even so, the very same word *bregando* is the example of language's quarrel with assaults it has been victimized by. Did I write quarrel? I wrote quarrel, I wrote scolding, I wrote punishment, I wrote revenge. That churning that attacks—between sentences—someone who speaks, those guttural sounds that substitute a well-turned expression, that pathetic adherence to the crutch of the word *bregando,* these are the punishments enacted by language against the onslaughts it's had to withstand. And worse still, the none-too-subtle scolding which leaves a person with their mouth wide open, dumbfounded.

Before we said a clever and waggish grafting. Now we say a grafting by European fathers. This phrase sums up the fear of Mother Africa that the anachronistic Puerto Rican has, who swears on the memory of Odysseus, that all of his ancestors, all of them white, *bregaron,* in the *Peloponnesus.* The anachronistic Puerto Rican, claiming to be an Atticist or a Celtiberian, hasn't found out that the *Peloponnesus* where his ancestors were *bregando* was a ramshackle little dive run by black folks in the old Santurce neighborhood of *Culo Prieto* (Black Behind). This sets the tone, like in the improvised *decimas*[14], in order to continue *bregando.*

Any kind of *mestizaje* implies transgression. Cultural, social, ethnic or racial, every *mestizaje* provokes the guardians of purity to go on a terrifying offensive. They fanatically point out this *mestizaje* as being provocative and dissolute, disrespectful and threatening. *Mestizaje,* which is the supreme Latin American triumph, responds defensively. And it confirms itself, spreads out its wings, diversifies itself, and becomes self-assured. Perhaps the original etymological *mestizaje,* along with the originality that the shaping *mestizaje* of what is uniquely Puerto Rican bestows on it, is what explains the self-assuredness and the diversification, the opening up and out and the confirmation of what *bregando* here is all about. But in the name of the three paragraphs needed to round out this task, what, in short, does *bregando* mean?

It means trying to wheedle your way out of misfortune. Like when you say that little Ivette is *bregando* with her mother's "Rita Hayworth illness," *bregando* with her father's boozing and her brother's sweet fascination for doing nothing. It means getting the most mileage you can out of happiness, or the appearance of it. Like when you whisper that Dalila is *bregando* with an old gamecock breeder who takes her to cockfights on Saturdays and Sundays, but on Tuesdays they go to *La garida del pirata* restaurant in Palo Seco and on Thursdays they eat at the *Metropol* in Isla Verde. It means to ritualize clandestinity. Like when it is rumored that Tito Quiquiriqui is *bregando* with a sugar daddy who buys him expensive shirts and perfumes him with "Obsession" and "Halston." It means to kick a bad habit. Like the comments about Pepe, the son of Don Pepe and Dona Pepita, who is *bregando* to get rid of drugs and attending evangelical faith-revival meetings. It means dealing with life's rip-offs. Like when they say that Mon Pipa's *bregando* with a salary that turns to salt, nothing. Isn't it odd that salt has gone down to nothing, when a long time ago it was a form of currency?

Bregando means trying to stay on top of it, to impose one's will by sweating it out or by subterfuge, by genuine effort or by playing the fool. *Bregando* means "I'm rooting for me," said with the cheerful ugliness that is so purely Puerto Rican. A place, I beg forgiveness, where impurity is the only pure thing, necessarily.

Like some people, the word *bregando* has many faces; many faces that speak of intransigent acts and clever deeds, many faces that conceal intimate processions and ambitions disfigured by humble vanity. We have to see these many faces of *bregando*, and of many people, with pity. But not that sort of Lite pity that some churches serve their customers, like the Madrid-type pity of St. Sebastian, with two faces. Yes, with the pity that recognizes imperfection as the most salient of human characteristics. Yes, with the pity which is *bregando* with all kinds of misery. Spiritual misery, social misery, moral misery. Miseries found in pajamas and a three-piece suit, in the mask and the face revealed, in the public apology and the private accusation, in the millions of daily mediations that language makes possible. One pertinent and formida-

Bregando

ble example of mediation is the sumptuous and overwhelming, the ubiquitous and democratic word *bregando,* with which, up to this moment, we've been *bregando.*

Translated by Alan West.

VISION, MYTH AND POWER
NATIONALISM AND
LATIN AMERICANISM

POETICS AND POLITICS IN LATIN AMERICA

JULIO ORTEGA

Since colonial times, Latin American poetry has been a political act, whose complex, even peculiar nature belongs more to the order of culture than to that of pragmatics. José Lezama Lima wrote, for example, that the first Cuban poem was actually a recipe a Spanish cook had sent back to Spain. The search for a new taste through a "mixture" of language and spices portrayed an inadvertent but meaningful act of reverse conquest. As Lezama points out, the 17th century Spanish baroque was the art of the Counter Reformation, and Latin American baroque was that of the Counter Conquest.

In the 1920s, the brilliant Brazilian avant-gardists founded the group Antropofagía in honor of the Indians who captured, cooked and ate the Portuguese bishop who intended to incorporate them into the ranks of Catholicism. The Indians incorporated the bishop instead, says Haroldo de Campos. His name was Sardinha, and that is what he literally became...

The first Peruvian poem was a satirical couplet of political denunciation. Because of factionalism, Peruvians conceived political discourse as indictment and disbelief. Mexico's first poems, on the other hand, were versions of the vanquished: chronicles that accounted for the dead and dying.

Writing in Latin America, then, began as a political activity. Written language in Latin America began as an instrument of power, legitimation and punishment. But while the rulers were confiscating the gold and the goods, the Latin Americans were controlling the processes of writing, recording, preserving and restoring. The result was a new culture built on a sign-system of exchange, resistance and the continuous incorporation of new objects and meanings. Written language, thus, became the backbone of the Latin American image. As Borges once stated, the Latin American writer moves freely beyond European national traditions and, therefore, combines at will a variety of styles and forms. Politics recatalogs this extensive repertoire from the perspective of a new culture.

In the 17th century the Peruvian Garcilaso de la Vega wrote a story about two Indians in charge of delivering melons from their masters to a nearby town. Although they had never tasted melons and were curious to try one, they were afraid of being seen by the letter they were carrying for their master's friend. The Indians didn't read or write, but they knew that reading and writing were the power of the rulers. The road was long, the day hot, and one of the Indians had an idea: to hide the letter behind a rock and satisfy their curiosity for this unusual fruit. Later, they ate a second melon. But when they arrived at their destination, the master's friend screamed, "This letter says you should have brought me eight melons! Two are missing! You will be punished!" And they were, convinced of the supernatural power of writing. The political subtlety of this fable underscores the new functions of signs, roles and values in Latin America. Despite the fact that the Peruvian Indians had successfully cultivated this exquisite fruit from Spain, they had been unable to taste the product of their own labor. They were as ignorant of writing as they were of that new taste.

Writing continues to be a decisive component of the cultural definition of Latin American identity and is exemplified by the works of Rubén Darío, César Vallejo, Pablo Neruda, Octavio Paz and Ernesto Cardenal, to mention poets of distinct political experiences. Yet if this identity carries a new intonation to the voices that demand our attention, that intonation is one of permanent questioning. Political consciousness is also made of poetic urgency. Poetry has often been the source of communal life in Latin America.

At the end of his life and when the Spanish Civil War was certainly lost for the Loyalists, Vallejo wrote:

Children of the World

If Spain falls—I mean, it's just a thought—
if she falls
(. . .)
children, how are you going to stop growing!
how the dipthong will remain in downstroke. . .!
How you're going to descend the steps of the alphabet
to the letter in which pain was born!

(translated by Clayton Eshelman)

To lose the meaning of one's political history is to renounce writing, to abdicate one's identity. Writing permits us to control our destiny, to shape it according to our demands.

In his recent poem, "Nieve de Provo" ("Honest Snow"), Chilean poet Gonzalo Rojas writes:

Bloody blood, who said the word blood.
Of that Franco who was
what was left but dirty incense smelling of blood.
Of this other *imbunche*, not even that, Allende:
the people are not for sale.

Imbunche is a monster from a Chilean myth. His body is totally covered with hair and he emits only guttural sounds; he eats human flesh and is a witches' patriarch. The *imbunche* in this poem is General Pinochet. From the images of a culture, the political dimension of poetry thus emerges.

Translated by C. Elliott.

QUESTIONS FROM THE AUDIENCE

Question: I'd like to ask whether Julio knows something more about the close relationship between "saber" and "sabor." Where does it come from, and how did it happen?

JO: Well, it is very difficult to know where it comes from, but in the first texts about Latin America there is an enormous curiosity about the new tastes, flavors found in the Indies. Columbus talks in his diary about the large fruits in the Indies and the gigantic trees, and clearly the knowing, the representation and even naming the new things entailed the necessity to try them, eat them, cook them, right? That is why the idea of the *locus amenus,* the lost paradise, after all, became a new theme in America at the beginning of these texts; it is what might be called "the place of abundance," or rather where things abound. The plants are enormous, the fruits larger, everything seems more abundant and more generous and proliferating in Latin America. And little by little it was going to happen that the new things of the Indies no longer enter into the register of vision and of naming, or rather within the laws of perspective and description known in Europe. So another language became necessary for those new things; that's how baroque language arose, as the language of exuberance, of proliferation, etc., as characteristic of American representation. That's also why, as Lezama Lima says, the baroque has a political connotation.

So "saber" and "sabor" are two operations of the same activity which is to know, classify, process, preserve, etc., that are definitions of cultural activity.

Question: Could "oler," to smell, also be included with "saber" and "sabor"?

JO: It's possible, why not? I do not recall any direct testimony about "smell," but knowing something by means of the senses is a privileged activity of the mentality of the 16th and 17th century, a mentality that believed experience to be the source of knowledge, right? And that is why, while the medieval world saw nature as given, made, defined by divine will, no doubt the discovery of America showed that nature is evolving, not yet finished, still being created. By the same token, man was also not yet finished. People are products of mixing, of cross-breeding, of the cultures that are made and re-made, and the great model of culture is nature, which grows, proliferates, never stops. This idea appears in the Inca Garcilaso de la Vega, for example. It is a political vision since in the face of the ethnocentric centralist European cultural vision which believed it possessed all the definitive models of reality, the Inca Garcilaso, Guamán Poma, the American chroniclers, were demonstrating every day that reality cannot be classified, that language is not sufficient, that experience demonstrates that things are new and different. And, therefore, that America is a reality that is changing the way of seeing, trying, knowing; changing our sense of the flavors and tastes of the world. After all, America was discovered in a search for spices, right?

Question about the relationship of language to identity: how has the Spanish language been affected by America?

JO: A new language does not invalidate an identity, but broadens it. Latin American culture shows that when the American peoples incorporated new languages, they developed with them and took power over them, as keeps on happening today. They assumed power over all of the formal instruments, all the European cultural models. Culture is, by definition, interchange, right? And a healthy culture is the one that makes the most interchanges, and which is broadened with those new incorporations.

Well, there is a lot of talk about indigenous languages, but that is another problem, it is a problem of who dominates in the countries, of who decides which are the writings that are desirable, scholarly and necessary. But what we call Latin American culture, which is a product of indigenous and European cultures, is, I believe, a development, an expansion of those elements thanks to the incorporation of European elements. Without that incorporation, the native Latin American cultures would have simply been dominated in all aspects, and the people would have simply been a work force. Clearly, many were that, and nothing more; they were exploited. But we would say that what we call Latin America today, which is a metaphor, clearly is a different culture within western culture, and that the difference comes from the origins which it passed through and which were processed by the native, aboriginal cultures.

There are obviously political forces which control the cultural spaces, and which impose models and versions that are not different from those used by the Spanish conquistadors, and the 500th anniversary of the discovery is a good example because the Catholic Church (not to go farther afield) is planning a re-evangelization of Latin America because of the anniversary, which is clearly calling for cultural ethnocide, right? But the Catholic religion in Latin America is very different from the official Roman Catholic religion...

Well, there are different efforts. For example in the Andean countries at the moment, there is a tremendous effort to recover, formalize and preserve the oral memory, because often their texts are oral and that's it. In Mexico also there is of course a great tradition of preserving oral cultural documents.

Borges said that the popular poet always seems very cultivated, very formal and at times that is true. But the interesting part is that the popular poets take possession of the classical forms of the Spanish tradition, make them their own and turn them into something else, and that is so very typical of the mechanisms of incorporation, of transculturation, or of the incorporation of a formal European code into the proper native expressive needs. So that the code is no longer what it was, it has become something else. And we see the same thing in religion; for example in Perú there is a god called Adaneva, an indigenous god called Adaneva that is clearly Adam and Eve (Adán y Eva in Spanish) and there is another legend, from the jungle of Perú, that says "the first man was a woman;" I think that is terrific.

Question about writing and the preservation of cultural identity in Latin America.

JO: ...I had simply forgotten, by my own fault, some women poets who are very important. For instance Alfonsina Storni and Gabriela Mistral, and Rosario Castellanos are poets who are preoccupied with the idea that writing must, in addition to many other functions, act to preserve. I believe that cultures are defined by the way they preserve, isn't that true?

We in this culture—a developed, technological culture—preserve by way of the computer. The data base and the diskette are extraordinary ways of preserving; also refrigerators and freezers, that serve to preserve the cultural information that we call food.

In other cultures they use ice, and complicated forms of preserving. Things last according to the ability that the culture has to preserve them. The wisest cultures are those that preserve things longer, those that consume a more durable information. We, since we are the victims of trends, consume very rapidly, and dismantle things because we need new things. But among poets: what are they seeking to preserve? They seek to preserve the notion of identity, by means of language, notes, signals; the common source of the culture as a space of identity. Where is the identity? In the community (*comunitario*), and the community, the notion of the community, is not something given, but something that is produced every day. Within the community is the identification with the Other, the idea that the Other forms part of the dialogue in which I am involved and which defines me. So then the Other is the one who defines me, because together we form part of the community.

I believe that in Latin American poetry—especially in the poetry of Ernesto Cardenal—one can see the valuation of the community as the space of the legitimation of the I, thanks to the Other, or rather this space of the Dialogue. That's why Ernesto Cardenal in his poetry, more than any other Latin American poet, is so concerned about the value of words. The precision of words. The critical capacity of words, or rather the possibility that words say the truth, the most difficult thing of all to do. And that's why in his poetry he criticizes slogans so much, the political manipulation of language, the publicity speeches, Hollywood superproductions—for example in the poem about Marilyn Monroe, which confuses reality with the inversion of dreams, prefabricated dreams—his preoccupation with language is, I believe, an almost ritual function of the civil poet, the poet who believes that the word community is the word we need.

Translated by Cola Franzen.

MYTH, LANGUAGE AND POLITICS

ALAN WEST

The bleak fate of Latin American writers has often been summed up in three words: *encierro, destierro* and *entierro:* jail, exile and death. *Encierro,* aside from the image of jail, also means being locked up in one's own thoughts, one's own world, cut off from the pulse and images of the streets. Hunger, illiteracy, censorship, repression and state-sponsored terrorism engender these three fates, and writers, like many others, respond: with cunning, imagination, courage and a strong dose of *locura.*

Resistance to these man-made disasters confronts a writer with his or her society's limitations, languages and myths. This is true even for writers who do not personally experience *encierro, destierro* or *entierro.*

LANGUAGE

An observant poet has noted "that when society becomes corrupted, the first thing that is gangrened is language." Prisons are called "La Libertad" ("Freedom"); "democracy" means if you don't agree you disappear in the night; "unfettered" or "free" markets means unbridled exploitation, huge concentrations of wealth in the hands of a few, and unemployment. There's more:

"Freely Associated State" becomes a euphemism for colony, and even here in the United States "freedom fighters" is used to designate a band of thugs who murder civilians.

But language having gangrened does not elicit the same cure as in medicine. You cannot simply amputate words from a language; it's been tried, and has failed miserably. No, it's the much more difficult task of recharging cultural thinking and expression by giving it back its true power, where literature plays an important function in trying to hold back the ravages of oblivion and indifference.

But holding back oblivion or indifference is not enough. There must be a vision to slice through the plague that has affected language, to slice through the discredit and effacement that words are submitted to. A way that will make expressiveness etch itself clearly, ideas flex themselves like shafts of light, so that words and new circumstances will collide, send sparks flying, bring us closer to ourselves.

Here's a look at my ongoing struggle with this vision:

> Language is a play of signs
> that takes us to other signs
> and so on.
> No, language is a superstructure
> where ideology can be read like
> a neon sign in Times Square.
> No, language is a spiral which
> contradicts itself like a vampire before
> the very same mirror, leaving traces
> which are barely audible.
> No, language is the varied repetition
> of one sole sound which masks us.
> No, language is a bullet pointing
> towards the future.
>
> So, what's the upshot?
>
> Language is everything, particularly
> if we do without words.
> Language is nothing, if, above all,
> we have bad aim.

Myth, Language and Politics

MYTH AND POLITICS

Myth, like politics, is a type of speech, a system of communication. We are surrounded by both to such an extent that it is often difficult to separate the two.

Myth has a relationship to language which is both parasitic and ravaging. Parasitic because it feeds off of an existing language in order to create itself, and ravaging because it takes that already-existing system of signification and turns it into highly-charged speaking corpses. Why corpses?

It is the mythic course to take what is full of meaning and strip it of its history, its richness, and change it into gesture. It takes anything remotely complex or ambiguous and turns it into something natural or eternal. As Roland Barthes said, "Myth does not deny things, on the contrary, its function is to talk about them; simply, it purifies them, it makes them innocent, it gives them a natural and eternal justification, it gives them a clarity which is not that of an explanation but that of a statement of fact." By organizing a world without contradiction, myth establishes a society without depth, where everything is self-evident, where things mean something by themselves, in an euphoric clarity. (Barthes)

Myth, then, distorts meanings and realities. Poverty, however unfortunate, is natural since it has always existed. Violence is abhorrent since it threatens the order of society. When it is used by the State to suppress strikes or demonstrations or to prevent a revolution, it is an act of self-defense, a call to restore national security, the "natural order of things." Myth is a depoliticized form of speech (Barthes), one that ruling classes have perfected to a greater or lesser degree in order to maintain a system of euphoric clarity. To question that euphoria is considered dangerous, and in Latin America that questioning can invite a murderous response.

MYTHS, COUNTER-MYTHS, PROPAGANDA AND WAR

Myths, in order to maintain their euphoria, often have to invent counter-myths. In Latin America the most dangerous of counter-myths is that of communism. And communism becomes the antithesis of fatherland, freedom, family, private property and—why not?—virginity. A huge system of propaganda is brought into place, the most monstrous example being Nazi Germany. More sophisticated versions exist and there's no doubt that the world of capitalist advertising is a much more clever presentation of myth and magic in a glittering anti-communist package. But when that fails, however, torture, jail, disappearance and murder are used. It's curious but not accidental that anti-communism's myths are elaborated around very abstract terminology: free enterprise, democracy, national security, nation and flag; but when it asserts authority, it does so by punishing the body either by starving it, limiting its movement (jail), torturing it, disappearing it or killing it. This is anti-communism's fundamental hypocrisy; in talking about freedom, order and prosperity it structures society for war, and views every act of independence as a tactical maneuver on a battlefield.

And yet at the same time that it wages its war, this anti-communist fever must drain that war of political significance and here is where torture and disappearance play a major role. It must make these ghastly actions a personal or family tragedy, and there can be nothing more personal than pain or the vanishing of a loved one. Torture, more than just inflicting pain, aims to accomplish something more ambitious: the unmaking of a person's world and values by destroying their trust in everything, by humiliating them to the point that their own words will betray someone else and themselves. A disappearance is horrifying, because it makes a loss irretrievable because if you mourn this act publically you run the same risk. You are left with two alternatives: silence, or you are compelled to speak in the way they want you to speak.

TAUTOLOGY AND THE VOCABULARY OF DEATH

But maintaining this magic and euphoria exacts a price: it turns public discourse into tautology. As Barthes said, tautology is a double murder: you "kill rationality because it resists one and it kills language because it betrays one." Tautology can only take refuge behind authority and "have a profound distrust of language, which is rejected because it has failed." And any refusal of language is like dying: "Tautology creates a dead, motionless world." Which is why this tautological society creates a huge vocabulary of death: pacification, neutralization, elimination; do away with, put an end to, dispatch; labor camp, development poles, strategic hamlet, deactivate undesirable elements; and so forth.

How to deal with these myths, with this proliferation of tau-

Myth, Language and Politics

tologies? Not all myths are negative or oppressive, just like the abuse of language doesn't mean that we have to abandon using words. We have our Macondos, our Salvador Allendes, our Ché Guevaras, our Comalas, our Leonel Rugamas, our Haydée Santamarías and our Frida Kahlos. But there's nothing dead about them because they are part of history, one that not only shows bravery and idealism but disappointment, pain, suffering, doubt and even weakness.

OUR MYTHS OF IMPURITY

To think their greatness is tarnished by their sensuality, their vision by their foibles, is to fall prey to the idea of myth as purity. Not only do we not need that kind of purity, we soundly reject it. I prefer Nicolas Guillén's definition:

> and I drink rum and beer and firewater and wine
> and I fornicate (even on a full stomach)
> I'm impure, what do you want me to say?
> Totally impure.
> However,
> I think there are many pure things in the world
> which are nothing more than pure shit.

Our literature is mythic in that we have taken the Spanish language and done with it what no Spaniard could ever dream of doing; our history is mythic in that we have taken our Spanish, Indian and African blood and written a new history with it; our political reality is mythic in that we have taken the *guaraní* myths, African religions, Christianity and Marxism and made them into revolutions. African slaves used church bells to play their Yoruba chants and communicate to their brother and sister slaves, unbeknownst to their Spanish masters. Give us a bell, a stick, a word, a bird or the earth and we will make it sing in sounds and images until the only myth will be the distant memory of *entierro, destierro* and *encierro*.

Alan West

QUESTIONS FROM THE AUDIENCE

Question about the relationship between oral and written language as a means of communication.

AW: Well, in the case of Cuba, we have always been very talkative. And they say that we talk a lot of shit too, right? But yes, a very strong oral tradition has existed in Cuba, and I believe there are strong oral traditions in all the Latin American countries, which is, I believe, due to a couple of things. At one time there was no television, and the way for people to communicate was through a public discourse outdoors or, once there was radio, to do it over the radio; and there was censorship, so some things couldn't be aired. Then the most effective form of communicating was to stop somewhere, form a group, and launch into a discourse or dialogue.

Obviously, the case of Fidel Castro is the case of an orator of mythical proportions (and many other dimensions); I was going to bring today the famous photograph of one of his first speeches after the Revolution, when he was speaking and behind him was Camilo Cienfuegos and all of a sudden two doves came, and one lit just beside the microphone and the other landed on Fidel's shoulder. Incredible, right? And there it is, caught in a photograph; it wasn't invented by anybody.

Question about whether the Latin American tendency to mythify reality and people has hurt more than helped.

AW: I believe that is true, that we have a tendency to mythify in what I call the pure sense of myth. What we have to keep seeing is how to elaborate more impure myths, and that means how to see things with a little more historical perspective; that's why I chose to mention people like Haydée Santamaría who was a great fighter, who ended her life very sick and with psychological problems, and committed suicide. Yet she will always be a great revolutionary, and at the same time a human being and not a myth, somebody of flesh and blood. Yes, we tend to project myths, to convert things into something else, make them divine and pure, and I believe that we have to go in the other direction. That's why I tried to elaborate some myths that would not blind us too much, because myth is necessary; I believe that a society cannot function without myths. They are a form of communication, and communication has to exist in every form of society.

TRANSCRIPT OF REMARKS BY ALFREDO JAAR

I am an artist and if I had to define myself based on the concepts of vision, myth and power, I could say that I don't believe in myths (and on the contrary I'd try to destroy all of them), and I have a vision, a personal one, but informed by public events, and that's why my work deals with the real world. And finally I hope my vision—which is my work, which is my art, which is also my voice—I hope my voice will be heard. And if that voice is heard, that's power.

I'd like to show you some slides of a project I did recently, called "A Logo For America." The project consists of a 45-second animated film, which I had the extraordinary opportunity to broadcast in Times Square in New York City on a big Spectacolor sign. This film was shown every six minutes, 24 hours a day, for one month; that's around 7,200 times, and I guess that's one way of getting heard. The concept of the project deals with the power structure that frames the relationship between this country and the rest of the American continent. This country has co-opted for itself the name "America," and even our everyday language forces

Alfredo Jaar
"A Logo for America"
1987
Computer animation, Spectracolor lightboard
Times Square, New York City

Transcript of Remarks

us to picture only one dimension of America. America unfortunately has been transformed into a word-image of the One that defines itself by exclusion of the Other. So this project demands the simplest kind of recognition, that is, of being put on the map.

...The piece starts with the map of the U.S.

...And then this map fades into just the outline of the U.S.

...And then the text, "this is not America" is overlaid on top of the map.

...And this refers to the fact that there's nothing more shocking, for myself as a Chilean or for any Latin American, to arrive in this country and be transformed into a "Hispanic" or a "Latin;" you have kept "American" for yourselves, so this text is referring to that fact.

...Then it moves to the flag of the United States.

...Then an outline.

...And then another text, "this is not America's flag."

...Then the word "America" starts growing on the screen.

...The letter "R" fills in.

...And then, the two elements of the "R" rotate; the half circle turns and the triangle also.

...Then by animation (remember all this is animation), the "R" transforms itself little by little into the map of America.

...Suddenly this map becomes two and moves toward both sides of the screen and erases the word "America."

...And then the two Americas come back into the screen.

...And become one again, at the center.

...Then this map of the American continent starts rotating—a reference to "North" and "South," to "top" and "bottom," to "us" and "them," "down there," the "back yard" and so on.

...And little by little the word "America" starts coming up and going down on both sides.

...And then it ends with the title of the work, "A Logo For America."

...And then my name appears; they forced me to put a name on it because otherwise it could have been confused with advertising.

Alfredo Jaar

QUESTIONS FROM THE AUDIENCE

Question about Jaar's use of English, rather than Spanish, during his talk.

AJ: I introduced my work by saying that it is very important to have power, and the only way to have power is to be heard. And those of you who speak Spanish in a way are all converted, so I am not really talking to you, that's why I am speaking in English. We are on the same side.

Question about the public reaction to the project discussed.

AJ: It's very difficult to quantify. There were many kinds of reactions. The most important was that of National Public Radio, which did a six-minute story about the piece. The journalist interviewed people on the street in front of the sign and asked questions. Some people said that the idea of the piece wasn't true, that it was illegal, and so on. I went there every other day just to watch; it's very difficult to quantify. Sometimes I thought of stopping people and asking what they thought, but that's not the point. But doing this piece was important for me. I've been here seven years and it was very important to make a statement of that kind. I resent the fact that we have been blurred into this "backyard" thing, we have no names, no identity, and we have become anything else but "Americans."

Question about what the work was intended to accomplish.

AJ: I'm very pessimistic, it's too late. One of my projects included sending letters to the editors of magazines, newspapers and TV asking why they use the word "America" to refer to this country and not to the continent. My work asks questions. I really don't have the answers, and I'll find out at the end of my life if I received any answer but I'm very pessimistic. The language is simply a reflection of the reality that's out there. In order for the language to change, the reality has to change. The power relations between the countries in the continent have to change; if those relations don't change, the language is going to stay the same. Language is a perfect reflection of what's happening, and when they say "This is America," this *is* America.

NATIONALISM AND
LATIN AMERICANISM

IDENTITY AS WOMEN?: THE DILEMMA OF LATIN AMERICAN FEMINISM

MARTA LAMAS

Latin America is a historical unity. What characterizes our plight is a common history of dependence, high rates of misery and exploitation, as well as a permanent struggle for independence. The similarities between Latin American countries derive from the economic and political models imposed on them, since their internal differences are quite profound. For starters, the multi-ethnic and pluri-cultural reality of Latin America is surprising: currently there are about 410 aboriginal ethnic groups, and there are varying degrees of *mestizaje*, resulting from the mixture of indigenous, African and European cultures, bringing about national identities distinct to each country. On the other hand, income distribution and the standard of living are in dramatic contrast: from Argentina to Nicaragua, from Guatemala to Venezuela, from Bolivia to México, from Brazil to Paraguay, the differences are enormous. And that's without mentioning the internal contrasts between the more industrialized zones and rural, poverty-stricken areas within each country; or the cultural and economic distance between the elite who enjoy the benefits of development and the great masses of the dispossessed, who barely subsist using the crudest methods of agricultural labor. This distance is so great that in most cases it would seem that we are speaking of two different countries.

It's obvious that the shared history of Latin America has had particular ramifications for Latin American women, whose oppression is a mix of long-standing cultural traditions, religious influences and *machismo*. In almost all Latin American countries the law stipulates equality between men and women. However this is a mere formality, with little effect on the daily lives of women. In fact, Latin American women are second-class citizens in their countries: their participation in the political process is virtually nil, and they also lack equal access to basic needs like education, health and employment. The highest rates of illiteracy and malnutrition are among women. Maternal mortality rates, due to inadequate care during childbirth and poorly-performed abortions, have yet to be eradicated. While governments support or impose family planning programs, they refuse to legalize abortion, out of fear of antagonizing the Catholic Church.

Latin American women who work outside the home face a common type of discrimination: the great majority have access to only "women's work," which implies a lower pay scale than men's. As domestics, cleaning women, secretaries, prostitutes or nurses, they have no avenues open to demand "equal pay for equal work." And even in those few positions where these demands can be voiced, you frequently hear the rationale that women work "to help out their husbands." In addition, housework is a full day's work in itself since there are no appliances, and few resources available. For the immense majority of Latin American women, being a *woman* means being responsible for the survival of a family under crisis conditions, bereft of social options that would enable them to combine household work with employment outside the home. With the [socio-economic] crisis, millions of women have had to go out on the street to seek an income. These "head of household" women, who take on the emotional and economic function of mother and father simultaneously, are constantly harrassed sexually in their workplace, and thousands have been raped. Young women are especially vulnerable to this predicament, aside from suffering unemployment and lack of job options and/or training.

The crisis has aggravated the living and working conditions of Latin American women. The feminization of poverty is increasing. The two characteristics of this division [of labor] are: the unrecognized/invisible work in the home; and, the confinement of working women to the feminine ghetto of low pay. For lack of collective solutions to child care and domestic work, women have had to bear this responsibility individually.

Under these kinds of exploitation and women's oppression, how do Latin American feminist movements surface? What are its defining elements and characteristics? I'm not going to go over the entire history, since in many countries organized feminist groups appeared as early as the turn of the century. I'm only going to refer to the new feminism which began around 1970. This resurgence is basically a phenomenon of a wider dissemination of feminist viewpoints. In Latin America, the first groups of new feminists were made up of women influenced by the publications and news being made by international feminism, especially by Latin American women exiled in the U.S. or Europe, who served as an international network. Hundreds of Latin American women felt an identification with the basic tenets of the new "Women's Lib" movement and organized their first groups of consciousness-raising.

Becoming aware of what being a woman meant entailed viewing motherhood in a different way, not as inevitable destiny but as a choice. This feminist "contagion" was well-received by some individuals, groups or institutions interested in lowering Third World fertility rates. From the time of the World Conference of the International Year of Women (1975), many governments signed international treaties of non-discrimination towards women, modified many of their laws and opened their doors to public and private foundations, state agencies and religious institutions interested in channeling money towards women. But it's not so odd that the majority of programs targeted for Latin American women were of a Family Planning nature.

Although in the majority of Latin American countries there are philosophical and organizational antecedents to feminist organizing, they appear as isolated cases. It was not until 1970 that in Mexico, Argentina and Puerto Rico there was an organizational

Identity as Women

resurgence of the movement, greatly influenced by North American feminism. In the other Latin American countries, it was the celebration of the International Year of Women (1975) that gave more vitality to the discussion, and led to a more heightened awareness regarding specific women's issues. During that period in Peru, Venezuela, Colombia, the Dominican Republic and Brazil, there was a resurgence of international feminism's global ascent (1975-78). At that moment, feminism was discredited in most other Latin American countries. Seen as "agents of Yankee imperialism" by the left, as "criminal abortionists" on the right, and as "lesbian anti-males" by the mass media, Latin American feminists had to face a war of attrition in order to legitimize the movement. It was only in the 1980s that feminism in Latin America gained respectability, both politically and academically.

CHARACTERISTICS OF LATIN AMERICAN FEMINISM

It is difficult to generalize about the development of the movement in all of Latin America. However, I'd like to take the case of Mexico, not only because it is the situation I'm most familiar with, but because it is illustrative of what went on in other countries as well. From a quantitative viewpoint, Mexican feminism has not expressed itself with the vigor of the North American or European movements, nor has it been able to solve the demands around which it has mobilized. But for this comparison to be pertinent, we have to consider the context within which Mexican feminism developed. Some of the reasons for the absence of a strong feminist movement have to do with certain common aspects of the socio-economic and cultural realities of Latin America: the region shares a level of development where a strong sexual division of labor is necessary, a weak civil society that is heavily *machista,* paternalistic and/or authoritarian regimes, a wavering, atomized or clandestine political praxis of the left, an enormous influence of the Catholic Church and the absence of socially independent organizations, as well as the lack of a tradition of mobilization, participation and debate by the citizenry, especially by women. Mexico shares all of these characteristics with other Latin American countries.

If we analyze the Western feminist movements, we see that a key mobilizing element was the consciousness-raising brought about concerning the oppression around domestic work and the role of being a housewife. In México this did not occur, and although the feminist movement in each country had its particularities, I think all Latin American countries shared this difference with their non-Latina counterparts. To understand why, it's important to see that middle-class Mexican women—including those from the lower middle class and even working-class women—do not bear the burden of domestic work by themselves. This is why they could evade, relatively speaking, certain internal tensions that housework can generate, particularly among couples. Whether it's because they have a domestic or because their mother, their sister or another member of the family is there to help, Mexican [and Latin American] women can count on help—another woman—to act as a shock absorber for the wear and tear, the confrontations and the problems created by housework. This cushion made feminism's political proposal into a statement without repercussions in the lives of women who could be receptive to it, namely middle-class women. Counting on family help or maids, these women did not live through the process of rebellion and confrontation as did their European and North American sisters. Because of their class background, many of these feminists stayed trapped in a contradiction. With someone to take care of domestic work, it wasn't necessary to go out and struggle for day care or for social measures which would ease the burden of domestic work. They had the money to have a safe abortion and were more protected from violence and sexual harrassment out on the street or in the workplace. By not needing the movement as a vehicle to better their living conditions, many of these women lived feminism as something which didn't affect their daily lives. Their militancy was reduced to that of *conviction but not of necessity.* Their path through small consciousness-raising groups underlined more a discovery of themselves as women and their common plight as such, especially with regard to sexuality, than any organizational need. Over the long run, many women abandoned these small groups, some seeking other political options, the majority in search of developing themselves as individuals. For them, feminism became an instrument of analysis for personal development.

It was those women with a greater political interest in going beyond their own personal circumstances—also, mostly middle-class—that carried on with the feminist project, linking up their work with groups of women from lower-income sectors. Such is the case of CIPAF in the Dominican Republic, Flora Tristán in Perú, and various groups in México and Brazil. In these groups a class consciousness was emphasized, as was the need for working with workers and peasant women (*campesinas*). A relationship was established with other organizations of the left. Some members of these groups practiced a "double militancy," in feminist groups and political parties. Others came from the experience of Christian-Based Communities. Many were radicalized by feminist thought.

From this Latin American experience, there is a dominant tendency of what is called socialist or marxist feminism. Although there are radical and liberal feminist groups, they are a minority. One element that made the development of feminism more difficult in the early years of the new feminism was the situation of misery and exploitation also shared by men. Faced with the typical question of "How to put forth issues of gender in the middle of hunger, misery and exploitation?", this socialist feminist tendency was able to defend the validity of its perspective by going to the crux of women's daily lives and showing their specific oppression, be it patriarchal violence or gender-based exploitation. This has been the guiding principle of socialist feminist work, and although different approaches were taken in line with distinct conceptual frameworks, its common thread was to work among certain classes, from an identity as women, and the problems, needs and desires that women face.

Nowadays this "popular" or "socialist" tendency within Latin American feminism has the greatest political presence. And though there is a clearly-drawn convergence on concrete projects and shared viewpoints, there's no reason to believe that the groups display a homogenous outlook. Many of these groups have channeled their efforts towards opening up a political space and acknowledgement within the left. They have faced considerable obstacles. The struggles to disseminate a feminist perspective and certain demands of the movement have been difficult to achieve. In many other cases, confronting patriarchal attitudes of so-called "fellow travelers" has been more taxing than facing outright reactionary sexism. In México, for example, when feminists initially put forth demands related to abortion in 1972, the left accused the feminists of being "agents of Yankee imperialism." Seven years later, that same left presented a legislative motion for a feminist law to the parliament on Voluntary Motherhood. Although progress has been made, there is within the political realm in Latin America, both in governmental and opposition ranks, a viewpoint that feminism continues to be a threat that must be contained through the symbolic presence of a few women. This inclusion of some significant feminine figures is in order to demonstrate that there are no major obstacles to women's participation and that women need not organize on their own.

LATIN AMERICAN FEMINIST CONGRESSES

At the beginning of the 1980s there were feminist movements in almost every country of the continent, with a bevy of publications, documentation and information centers and with a wide variety of organizational forms. The need to get together and share experiences was felt. Acting on the initiative of the Venezuelan *compañeras,* the effort was undertaken to hold the First Latin American Feminist Conference in Bogotá, Colombia in 1981. There were 250 women representing the national variants of Latin American feminism and for several days they debated, trying to refine the discussion around two principal axes: sexuality and politics. As there was common agreement on a left perspective, the issue of a double militancy was the most discussed, especially in terms of the autonomy of the movement. In this meeting, despite open differences, Latin American feminists shared one common theme: anti-imperialism. What did (does) that mean? That Latin America's historical reality weighed heavily in the discussions. The struggle for national independence—political or economic—was ever-present in the debates. This meant that feminism was conceptualized as part of the process of transformation and liberation of each country and it seemed like there was a shared identity of being a *Latin American woman.*

Two years later, in Lima, Perú, the conference grew to 600 feminists. The central theme was "Patriarchy in Latin America." In Lima, a substantial step was made in the conceptualization of certain key themes such as power, patriarchy and whether there was anything like a "correct line," and the implications of a slogan like "Without socialism there is no feminism." In addition the Southern Cone was experiencing a democratic opening at that moment and this meant a reunion among exiles and those women who had remained in their respective countries.

In 1985, the Third Conference, in Bertioga, Brazil, marked a moment of consolidation. Close to 900 women took part. Among the highlights of the discussion were the political changes in the region and a series of themes previously left untouched by feminists, such as the relationship with the state and with public institutions. The stature of feminism among women's movements made it possible for the first time for there to be women present who did not openly define themselves as feminists (they were not numerous). There was also a confrontation between these women and feminists which garnered much press attention; a non-feminist group took a bus with women from the *favelas* (slums) right to the door of the conference and pressured the conference for the right to participate in the proceedings. When the feminists agreed to allow two women to come in as free participants, the women of the *favelas* insisted on "all of us or none of us." The conference was being held in a rented space that didn't have room for "all of us," nor was there money to sustain them for the five days. They didn't accept the practice of having representatives, so the "women of the people" did not enter. Although the incident caused a certain discomfort, all of the participants recognized that it was a case of political provocation.

The Fourth Conference was in Taxco, México, in 1987. More than 1,500 Latin American women were present, and with the exception of Panamá, Curacao, Belize and the English-speaking Caribbean countries, all of Latin America was in attendance. The central theme of discussion was "Feminist Politics in Latin America Today." What characterized this meeting—aside from organizational deficiencies—was the massive participation of women from non-feminist political organizations, militants of women's and popular movements, mothers of the disappeared, cadres from worker and peasant organizations, women from the Liberation Theology movement, women from exile groups and so on. For the first time Cuba sent an official delegation and there were a great many Central American women involved in the political and armed struggle of their countries.

Each conference has been a political event, and its stature and impact has each time led to a greater number of non-feminist women participating, something that feminism has traditionally desired. But this time there was a different situation. Although the other conferences encouraged women to discover feminism, in Taxco the number of non-feminists gave it a different dynamic. These women who had never participated in the feminist movement in their countries, many coming from those sectors of society that socialist feminists were interested in working with politically, *invaded* the feminist space, showing their restlessness and concerns—not always from a feminist angle—causing, in many cases, a repetition of previous debates. These women wanted to talk about what they were living through, important matters like the war in Central America. Without invalidating or belittling these issues, many feminists pointed out that the purpose of the conference was not being adhered to: discussing feminist policies and politics. This put the feminists in a bind: what to do if what these women wanted to debate and collectively clamored for as feminists were broad matters, not specific to feminism? Since there was a supposed self-initiating/managing process, each person gathered with others to discuss what they wanted to, with the limitations that this type of selective process entails. But the issue was brought to light.

THE DILEMMA FOR LATIN AMERICAN FEMINISTS

The dilemma for Latin American feminism has always been its relationship to women's movements. This relationship has been difficult, marred by mistrust, but also filled with a sense of discovery, questioning and supportiveness. And it seems like in Taxco a limit was reached concerning this dilemma. One could see that there are feminists who were no longer willing to continue debating what non-feminist women wanted to discuss, be it broad issues like sexuality or specific ones like the political situation of a given country. Many feminists asked themselves for the first time how to deal with the much-desired increasing influx of women in terms of the development of the movement. Undoubtedly, the richness derived from having so many and diverse women participating was a clear indicator of feminism's influence. But there's a need to take it further. It shouldn't be forgotten that many feminists were not pleased with the dynamics of the meeting. It's worthy of analysis, as is the label of "elitism" which was bandied about

Identity as Women

and counterposed to that of "populism," and both of these tendencies need more in-depth discussion.

In Taxco, once again, the movement's inability to deal with these disparities was revealed. Negating our differences has bogged down feminist politics in a kind of pseudo-egalitarian sisterhood (*mujerista*) discourse. Many feminists don't seem to identify with this discourse and yet they haven't dared to confront it. In the plenary session of the Fourth Conference all the attendees unanimously echoed the phrase "We are all feminists," raising doubts among those who have heard time and again, both in the debates and privately, "I'm not a feminist but. . ." What does this mean? More than a speedy conversion to feminism, it's a matter of the dynamics of mass movements, which sweep people along towards positions that individually they wouldn't take on. But this crisis of acknowledgement and identity also manifests the confused relationship between women's and feminist movements. It's not a question of saying that one is more legitimate than the others but of recognizing and coming to terms with the differences between them.

On the other hand, many Latin American feminists feel the need for a change in the internal dynamics of their movements, and of the conferences. In order to build a feminist movement that generates ideas and produces political transformations, it's not only important to struggle for disseminating feminist viewpoints—strengthening its relationship to the outside world—but also to struggle to create the internal conditions necessary for thinking and creating. It is all too rare to come together in one place in order to face these positions and to analyze the political practice that has been evolving. There is a dire need to get together and talk things through. In Taxco, this need was taken on by ten feminists: from Perú, Argentina, Chile and México. They locked themselves up to reflect in a systematic way on the theme of the meeting: feminist practice. For three mornings they talked, took notes and shared experiences from their countries. On the last day they hammered out a document to be presented at the plenary session and thus share the process they had gone through, and thereby "socialize" the information. This mechanism—working in a small group and arriving at conclusions—let them derive the maximum benefit that the conference allowed in being able to speak among themselves. None of them would have been able to come up with such a document in their own country, without the participation of the other women, or in an open workshop situation with 50 or so other women. For them it was decisive to be able to remove themselves from the *modus operandi* of the conference—"they can all get together and talk about what they feel like"— and take on the task of really being able to speak to each other in a more focused way.

In the document called "From Love to Necessity," they proposed a rupture with the "amorous logic" that was prevalent in feminism ("We all love each other, we are all equal") and instead proposed to recognize the need they had for other (non-feminist) women. They pondered external obstacles and internal bottlenecks in Latin American feminist political practice. Their analysis began by acknowledging what has been achieved: the place of feminism within women's movements in Latin America, the advances made from Bogotá to Taxco, the fact that popular, political, religious and academic organizations, as well as parties and even some governments have included feminist demands as part of their programs. The social and political legitimation of feminism is a given.

In comparing their experiences, they detected the existence of a mythology which criss-crosses their discourse. The common thread of this mythological system is *mujerismo,* the belief in an "essence" of women, which from the start tries to erase conflict, contradiction or difference. From this idealization of women, how do you confront the complacency, wear and tear, inefficiency and confusion that many feminists detect and realize are present in the majority of groups involved in feminist politics in Latin America?

There are some feminists who are aware that a consequence of sexual differentiation is not that women are better or worse than men. They don't start from an outlook that postulates an essence of "being a woman," but instead accept the fact that women's inequality stems from having lived immersed in material and symbolic misery and because women have not been granted much significance except as mothers; that is, they have not had social and cultural significance as human beings. Women's mediation with the world has consisted of being and living for others: love as a means of attaining significance (and of signifying).

This way of relating to the world has been brought over into the daily social and political practice by feminists, thereby developing a love-instilled rationale of "We all love each other, we are all equal," which doesn't allow for dealing with conflict and differences. To demystify this hodge-podge, we have to put an end to this amorous discourse and go on to a relationship of needs. Women need each other in order to have political strength. It's a matter of doing away with self-complacency, in order to break away from using a victim's discourse. From this perspective, there is a revision and theoretical exploration going on which places the political and symbolic consequences of sexual differentiation between men and women at the center of the debate. It's not a matter (as it was years ago) of destructuring a masculine culture, nor of opposing it with a feminist counter-culture, but instead of re-thinking human experience as one marked/deformed by being-woman/being-man; that is, marked by a sexual differentiation and also by the concrete political and cultural problems of each country.

In this debate there are common points which span the continent. Various Latin American feminist groups have put forth, for example, the need to define more clearly their relationship with the state and their participation in government programs. Others have a clear consciousness about the need to participate, *as a feminist movement,* in a process of consolidating a democratic option. This could mean anything from the building of a new party to a more organized participation within existing political organizations. Other feminists have decided to organize themselves around a struggle against the principle obstacles which prevent their participation as citizens on behalf of political democracy. The common objective in Latin America nowadays seems to be to obtain a partial and specific level of influence or bearing on how to solve the numerous problems that women suffer from on a daily basis. Undeniably, various feminist groups share the idea of a much wider political participation as a way of emancipating women. The discussion now centers on *democracy.* "Democracy in the country and in the home," as Chilean women said several years ago; but although it is a felt demand throughout Latin America, the Latin American feminist movement doesn't have a clear position on what democratization implies. The difficulty with various groups in participating to build a democracy also has to do with seeing feminism as a "revolutionary" option. Although there is agreement that a feminist concept of democracy should outright include the basic right of people to control their own bodies (from abortion to freely exercising one's sexual options), there is disagreement on a whole range of issues, one example being that of parliamentary participation.

One of the oldest and greatest challenges to the feminist movement still holds true for almost all of Latin America: to elaborate a political project which deals head-on with the contradiction between work and social reproduction. Although many movements have taken up the needs, hopes and desires of women and shaped them into concrete demands, this hasn't meant that the project for solving that contradiction has been created. The majority of women mobilize for "non-feminist" reasons: their disappeared sons and *compañeros,* issues related to running water, electricity, basic services and the high cost of living. With mounting social crises, the economic and social differences between women have increased. And though feminism proposes a united front to face *machismo's* oppression, the reality is that women forge class or ethnic alliances with men more readily than those based on gender. That is why the utopian vision of political unity among women has perished. There is no "natural" unity among women, it has to be built through political work. Now, a paradox arises from this situation: women need to acquire a specific consciousness about being women to be able to struggle later with male-female differences. This is a complex process with grave implications. Part of the price you pay for a politics so deeply rooted in consciousness and the affirmation of identity is isolation, and not being linked up to wider social movements. In addition, many women get bogged down in this process, staying submerged in *mujerismo,* without acquiring a feminist consciousness.

Feminism proposes to foment organizing women on their own, with a gender-based political perspective. How to achieve this without falling into *mujerismo?* This is, I believe, the challenge that confronts us as feminists in dealing with the dilemma of our relationship with women's movements.

Translated by Alan West.

DOES ART FROM LATIN AMERICA NEED A PASSPORT?

LUIS FELIPE NOE

THE PROBLEM IS THE PROBLEM

The issue of identity in Latin America is like the sword of Damocles, suspended over the heads of the artists in this part of the world. The sword will fall on the heads of those who don't want to deal with it. It is a logical concern, a reaction against cultural dependence on Europe and now, on the U.S. But, is our problem being correctly formulated in this way? I can understand that third parties—that is, people from the above-mentioned countries—will state the problem in this way because of their ignorance; they do it as a policeman who demands identification papers, or the bureaucrat who asks for your birth certificate. This attitude is the same as asking if Latin American art exists, and if it does, how does one define it?

This last question is absolutely totalitarian, for they know very well (and they defend this concept as a supreme value) that the collective realm is multifaced and pluralistic. I can understand our artists asking themselves, subjectively, *who are we?*, especially if this question arises from a new generation trying to situate itself polemically with regard to previous generations, as it ought to. This is all the more true, on the one hand, when its members feel challenged by a social destiny in formation; and it is more difficult to handle, on the other, because it creates a feeling of marginalization. In any case, it is in this way that the artist lays claim to his milieu, a fundamental endeavor.

But this issue of identity nurtures misunderstandings by cultural centers (either through disregard or lack of interest) which, in addition, are (and not by chance) also the political and economic centers. This misstatement of the problem of identity winds up validating the problem as a reality. The problem of identity in Latin American art appears to exist. But we should ask ourselves if the real issue is not another one entirely and, even worse, if in facing the problem in this manner, we simply shut it out altogether.

In order to decipher the mystery, let's first elaborate on a precise terminology for words such as art and identity.

THE PHENOMENON CALLED ART

I believe the complex phenomenon encapsulated in the word art is simply another vehicle for understanding the world, discovering its secret codes by means of a specific language. Such language—as opposed to rational discourse—is one which has not been codified previously. This holds true for all artistic languages, as they are sometimes nurtured by gestures, other times by musical signs, other times by visual elements and finally, by words; even though the model for codification is usually the language of words.

This is how poetry, in its condition of artistic thought, is decoded (and we already know that thought and language mirror each other). Poetry's semantic codes are established in tandem with the formulation of its discourse; these codes are also intimately related to codes discovered by the artist in his/her relationship with the environment. However when these clues are established as clues to a vision of the world, they are oftentimes mistaken for specific codes in already-determined artistic languages. This is how academic institutions are structured: to protect these codes as if they were laws, applicable in all cases.

The artist defines the environment—its range and characteristics —and, *who is s/he?* Simply, the one who practices this form of

Does Art From Latin America Need a Passport?

communication with his/her own milieu. This milieu consists not only of spectators, but basically of all the signs in the world which the artist wants to decipher and that evade him/her: the intermediate and the immediate, the apparently abstract and the apparently concrete. This milieu is simultaneously universal and particular. The artist, in relationship with both the surroundings and with the nature of language, particularizes universal themes and, insofar as particular themes can be transcended, the artist renders them universal.

THE ISSUE OF IDENTITY

The tackling of the question of identity in the realm of art is related to the language one employs in order to understand the surrounding environment. The artist becomes conscious of him/herself at the moment of assuming a language and a milieu, simultaneously. If the problem of identity is always an individual one, does it make sense to state the national identity as part of the field of aesthetic and cultural theory? In the case of Latin America there is an explanation which implies that this is not a logical approach. We should ask ourselves whether, since it is not logical, it is absurdly totalizing and totalitarian.

It is inconceivable for a European artist to harbor such a question. For Europeans it would be at a personal level, and this would suffice to reaffirm their membership in a country and a continent. For North American artists, on the other hand, the question arose at the moment of defining themselves *vis a vis* Europe. Nevertheless the assurance that comes with power led them to become aware of how unnecessary the question is. The answer was already given through the security that comes with exercising power. First Action Painting and, later, Pop Art manifested this in uneven ways.

Defining one's identity is a pertinent problem for an adolescent, who questions him/herself as a preamble to saying, "Here I am, and this is what I am." As s/he gains confidence, s/he no longer formulates the question, but simply *is*. The issue of identity is the result of the need to find a path to embark on. But the awareness of being oneself (in other words, identity) is the consciousness of being in becoming (this is why "There is no path; we make it as we journey").

However, we can understand this yearning for a national path (or for a Latin American one, for those who believe in a Latin American identity, as is more and more often the case); it comes from a feeling of marginalization in relation to what has been labeled as "universal art," a label that the centers of power impose upon us. It's a need for self-affirmation in facing the world. And although this attitude is not necessarily antagonistic, evidently it's not easy to synchronize with the humble tasks of artists as they decipher clues to the world, the essential artistic endeavor.

THE FEELING OF MARGINALIZATION
The feeling of marginalization brings our problem to an ontological level which can be summarized in the formula, "To be, or to be on (the) edge." In this way, the right wing nationalists from various Latin American countries have affirmed the existence of a "national entity," defined as Western and Christian, just the same as French right wing nationalists define themselves. The doubt-prone left responds to this with the problem of a "national identity," while many sectors exalt specific indigenous issues. Liberals, on the other hand, uphold the universality of culture; the ontological question, therefore, takes on a political definition.

Meanwhile, Edmundo O'Gorman[1] defines the American way of being (generically speaking) as the following: "Being as others, in order to be oneself." Leopoldo Zea[2] puts it this way: "Being like the others, in that which serves the will to be oneself; a relative renunciation, to achieve a reaffirmation of the most positive aspect of our being." Contrast this metaphysical candor with the diatribes of many artists against cultural dependence. We could call this reflection PanAmericanist, for it puts the U.S. and Latin America on the same level. If there is truth in this affirmation it will, curiously, be more applicable to the U.S., for they have built their power based on values derived from metabolizing European civilization.

But the Latin American art that was born from these ideas has always seemed, in general terms, to be bound to European influence and, now, to North American influence. I say in general terms because these are the terms in which we judge whenever the identity issue is questioned. For example, who cares to recognize that the will to enter the process of invention of contemporary art was actually born in Argentina, in 1946, with a group of artists

Does Art From Latin America Need a Passport?

who stated the problems and solutions in the visual arts, anticipating U.S. artistic trends by 20 years? I'm referring to the Madí group. The interest of some Argentinian critics in these breakthroughs has been just the opposite, with the exception of a few who recognized the originality of the group's statement, only after the "shaped canvas" came forth. Up until then, these same critics considered it a movement derivative of Europe's cultural activity. This is only one of many possible examples.

CULTURAL SELF-COLONIZATION

This referential mentality is studied in depth by the Argentinian painter and theorist Kenneth Kemble[3]. In his article, significantly titled "Cultural Self-Colonization," he reflects upon and cites numerous examples disproving critics who maintained that Argentina didn't produce any authentic artistic avant-garde movements.

He begins his study by reminding us of the story of Linnaeus: "They say of Linnaeus that when he found an insect which resisted classification, he would crush it immediately." In the case of the critics who disdained Argentina's creativity, they applied systems of classification that weren't even theirs, but borrowed from the central countries. These critics were behaving in a self-colonized way, taking for granted the validity of their up-to-date information on all cultural processes, in their exercise of power and establishment of value (in their hearts, they think this is "happening at home").

Whatever is ignored by the centers of power "doesn't exist." As a result, the centers despise whatever they refuse to know (which is not the same as saying that they do not know). All that escapes their interest in defining as valuable is put aside. And what do they recognize (because it's about this: a willingness to recognize) from the peripheral cultures? Whatever is similar to them, and hence recognizable, and which is, therefore, considered to be merely mimetic.

The self-colonized person responds to this attitude by conceding everything that the centers of power want, in order to reaffirm the colonial rationale. Do the colonialists want Informalism? We have it. Do they want Conceptual Art? We have it too. We even have Technological Art, even though we have no technology. The

Luis Felipe Noé

self-colonized will exemplify this attitude with works they choose to exhibit abroad, either by selecting coherent examples of "Latin American art," or by showing incoherent ones, bits of everything, if not of the worst. But is this a problem of cultural identity or of cultural self-colonization in our arts policies? What is evident is the fact that this is a way of self-effacement; if they disregard us abroad, they will be correct in doing so. Does this certify a real Latin American impotence in being able to achieve what Leopoldo Zea alludes to as "the most positive aspects of our being?" Does this mean that in the process of "being like the others, in order to be ourselves," we simply settle for being bad copies of others? Must we reject all external influence as pernicious, simply because it wouldn't let us be? Do we have to reject all previous Latin American history because it's marginal to the "true history of art" and only admit (recognizing their minor importance) those works which spice modernity with local anecdotes? What should we choose to paint between, for example, a representational theme that describes the terrible injustices and contradictions of social life, and an abstract painting nurtured by the pre-Columbian past? Or maybe we should ask ourselves, should we return to the source (as some believe), that is, to the primitive expression of art? But please, not inspired by the Altamira Caves, for they are located in Spain!

THE NATIONALITY OF ART

Perhaps what seems to be clearer is that the issue of national identity (or its repercussions) really involves all Latin America as a community of common destiny, in spite of nationalities. The differences among Latin American countries have been marked by pain, among the Hispanic, indigenous and immigrant roots. And, doesn't the answer for the problem of identity implicitly lie in the assumption of a common destiny? Isn't this assumption eliminating, at the same time, its own *raison d'être* by undermining the idea of national identity? I approached this problem in a chapter of my book *Antiaesthetics* (published in 1965) entitled "The Nationality of Art," by proposing three perspectives on the issue. These are:

1st: "It is widely said that art is international. This is not true. Art is national regarding creation, since man

Does Art From Latin America Need a Passport?

lives in a specific place and context. It is, on the other hand, international regarding results, for mass media makes it so." (...)

2nd: "The opposition between international avant garde art and our authentic art is an absurd one, because of its impossibility. It tries to oppose ideas that lie on different planes. It also tries to confront one truth of art, as it relates to time, with another, as it relates to space; when the fact is that the artist is located in both time and place." (...)

3rd: "The only way of becoming universal is through the reaffirmation of the particular; but, at the same time, the only way of seeing the particular is through a global perspective. Moreover, the universal is a dynamic process. The only way to deal with the particular is within the dynamic of the actual." (...)

Finally, I will relate this topic to a problem I find particularly important: the acceptance of a chaos that surrounds us as a latent order, one which must be understood and grasped and in which our preconceptions of the nature of order are worthless. Like a pot cover that can't cover a pot of larger diameter. "The Latin American chaos is still waiting to be undertaken. It's a whole reality that awaits, as if waiting to see its own face. Art, in finding this face, accomplishes its mission. A continent, an unmade society, awaits it. Like it or not, consciously or unconsciously, since it still ignores its destiny, society expects a revolution from art."

I believe there is a difference between speaking about the problem of national identity and dealing with the "nationality of art," the former being a recognition of both the conditioning cultural context and of the defiant presence of the artist's milieu. The second attitude supposes that nationality cannot be questioned, for it underlies everything. A nation is not an identical entity or an ethnic uniformity, but a common destiny, dictated by historical and geopolitical reasons. The common features cannot be demanded, only crafted. When I spoke about accepting and taking on the chaotic, I was referring to the divergent—to assume it is not necessarily to find in it a common essence.

POWER (TO) AND NO POWER (TO)

The so-called problem of identity, at the national level, is a reality as it pertains to the issue of marginalization and power (better still, no power (to)). No power to do what? To be in full liberty, to reaffirm values/ Hamlet's doubt (to be or not to be) is a vitiated form of addressing the awareness of not being a full human being.

On the contrary, the culture that arises from the centers of political and economic power simply "is," because it is able to. It doesn't hesitate about its power to be. It's a culture that behaves simultaneously as the actor and spectator of itself. It applauds itself and decides which values shall be universal.

The concept of marginalization and power lies within the political and economic geography, divided into metropolitan and peripheral countries. One of the consequences of belonging to the periphery is cultural dependence. We must take on this problem for what it is—for its intellectual nonsense and its corruptive power. But an artist cannot resort to solutions of orthopedic prosthesis (like demanding him/herself to work on themes and signs already concocted) in order to cease being dependent upon cultural centers.

The obsession with keeping up to the minute with whatever is done in the cultural centers of power (which always leads to being one minute late), together with academic prejudices, makes us forget that the function of the artist is to decipher the signs that elude us—signs that are present in the surrounding environment and from which the artist proposes new ways of seeing. But doesn't something similar occur to those obsessed with the problem of identity?

NOSTALGIA

Nostalgia is characteristic of people who are severed from their harmonic relationship with traditions (like the indigenous populations) and also of those who have moved in migratory waves (including those who defend the existence of a hispanic-creole past). Nostalgia, that distance from oneself, is not an ontological problem. Although it doesn't generate a unique identity, it does generate a culture rich in contrasts, baroque, fantastic or melancholic. Nostalgia is not always expressed as the harmful engine of self-colonization, for it can also create rather new ways of see-

Does Art From Latin America Need a Passport?

ing and feeling the world.

It is in this way that nostalgia has been useful to Argentinians, especially those who have been subjected to more external influence, to bring forth two visions of universal repercussions: the tango, and Borges' literature. These manifestations have a fundamental local precedent in the work of Macedonio Fernández, an Argentinian writer. The cultural vision of the world comes from a dialectic interrelationship between different contributions.

The artistic identity is something so inherent for someone who informs his/her cosmovision in their relationship to their milieu that I will give two examples that reverse the thematic premise: the perspicacious vision of a European, within Surrealism, Gertrudis Chale. Her interest projected into the *altiplano* and into the desolate suburbs of Buenos Aires. The same can be said of Lasar Segall, formed within the Expressionist School, about his interpretations of Brazil.

Symmetrically speaking, I remember that Sam Hunter said that the most penetrating vision of the American society of the 1960s arose from an artist of the same country, Andy Warhol and also from the Argentinian Jorge de la Vega, through a totally different perspective. The artist, in his/her vision of the world, has a right to refer to any theme and to any root. What artists don't have a right to do is renounce their responsibilities as artists by being "up to the minute," that is, by being self-colonized.

It's crucial to be aware that vision of the world is an artistic issue and not an issue that belongs to criticism (as it might seem from the fact that museum bureaucrats from metropolitan countries who visit Latin America hold preconceptions of the visions they expect from Latin American artists). If, before, they were looking for that which corroborated their own outlook (that is, what was fashionable), now, in this period of a crisis in creativity, they will try to entertain themselves with folkloric particularities that do not constitute a real threat to their own values. This doesn't mean that they respect and take into consideration such particularities; everything that is genuinely different they will discard beforehand.

The time will come when our artists will not need to present a passport—that document which testifies to their origin and identity—in order to be accepted in other countries. They will simply be accepted as artists. But, there is still an issue of power, difficult to solve, before this change can occur. The so-called issue of identity is in reality a problem of respect: respect among ourselves, and to be respected in return. For others it is an issue of learning to respect us, to simply let us be. But before that, there is a question of power that will have to be resolved.

Translated by Alan West and Cristina Cardalda.

PAINTING, IDENTITY AND THE PURSUIT OF HAPPINESS

WILFREDO CHIESA

As painters we are faced with a paradox; to visualize and render an image which will make us—and hopefully others—see and feel something which in a sense is not really there. Through technique and skill, we try to reach that most essential area of art which is experiential rather than visible. Our images, at their best, hope to obliterate the visual in order to deliver feeling. Then, we come to realize that the reality of painting lives within its own nature: in its flat surface, in its illusion of space. To face a painting we must give ourselves up to its magic, just as we enter the dark chamber of a movie house and for 90 minutes live other lives in other places. According to Cézanne, "nature lives within," and that "within" is what the painter has always sought.

Soon after finishing art school I abandoned representation and was lured by abstraction as a resource to explore that which we cannot see, in order to make it visible. Edgar Degas wrote: "A picture is something which requires as much knavery, trickery and deceit as the perpetration of a crime. Paint falsely and then add the touch of nature. The artist does not draw what he [sic] sees,

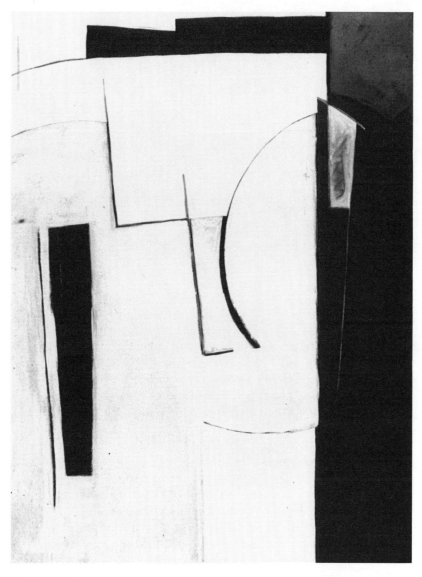

Wilfredo Chiesa
"Espacio Escondido"
1988
Acrylic on canvas, 80" x 66"

Wilfredo Chiesa
"Blanco Espana"
1987
Acrylic on canvas, 80" x 90"

but what he must make others see. Only when he no longer knows what he is doing does the painter do good things . . .The air we see in the paintings of the old masters is never the air we breathe."

In search of an Antillean image, I worked for some time with bleached-out, overexposed colors, typical of the Caribbean. Working within abstraction, those paintings dealt with issues of space and with shapes that made reference to that region's landscape. It was useless. I soon came to realize that any color is a tropical color when you look at it in the tropics. Thus I moved to a more formal kind of painting in which color issues became more personal, and pictorial activity concentrated on the exploration of shapes and spatial relationships as expressive visual metaphors. In the sequence that leads from one painting to another and to the next, an abstract painter, as well as others, uses the previous work as a sort of model to take off from, to manipulate and sometimes to reject. Painting, therefore, is never disassociated from the concrete world of the real since it uses itself (an object) as subject matter. Art, then, confirms the ambiguity of vision, and demonstrates that the line between illusion and authenticity, between fantasy and reality, is a thin one. In Latin America this line is not only thin, it is transparent.

In our countries, where metaphors outnumber computers, it is not strange to find a propensity toward metaphorical rather than scientific thinking. It is no surprise that much of our creative activity has been defined with labels such as "magic realism" or "art of the fantastic."

What is really magical and fantastic about painting is its ability to show us things which we may fail to see outside of painting, or which may not even exist!; to deliver an image, within its limited visual space, charged with emotional, political, spiritual or any other type of energy, in which we can mirror our visible or our invisible selves. When told that his portrait of Gertrude Stein did not resemble her, Picasso responded: "Someday she will look like my painting." It may be that skill and inspiration are two intertwined tracks in painting, but they are two tracks nevertheless. One is only good in support of the other. Johannes Itten reminded us: "theory was meant for moments of weakness."

Then, are Latin Americanism and Nationalism issues in my work? Does it matter? I hope that they aren't, and I hope that it

Painting, Identity and the Pursuit of Happiness

doesn't. I do not personally know any artist who is in any conscious way pursuing a Latin American or national image. We paint what we are, what we see, and mostly what we don't see. If the bond between art and identity is a strong one, so is the freedom of the creative process which leaves us open and vulnerable to a broad range of influences, both national and foreign, personal and universal. As contemporary urban beings we live more and more an inter-personal and inter-national reality. The existence of multiple cultures in our continent results in a plurality of identities as well as a plurality of images. Language aside, an Argentinian seems to me to be as different from a Dominican as a Dane is from an Italian. At art museums in the United States I have seen cards identifying El Greco as "Greek, worked in Spain," Picasso as "French, born in Spain," and Antonio Frasconi as "American, born in Uruguay." Is it a matter of passports? Are Paul Gauguin's Tahiti paintings French? Are Diego Rivera's cubist paintings Mexican? It seems to me that this is mostly a curator's or an art historian's concern. Ernesto Sábato in *Abaddón el Exterminador* said: "The dilemma is not between the social and the individual ...the dilemma is between what's frivolous and what's grave."

When we paint we are concerned with space, with color, with our visual voices. In the studio we still marvel as we spread color on a surface and it tells us something which we fail to express with words. We are enjoying ourselves, but we are also in despair for we know, as someone has said, that anything we paint can be used against us. A sadly true and horrifying thought. Yet, we keep on painting.

I will not respond to the question of whether there is a truly Latin American art. But I have witnessed a distinct Latin American public. Throughout our countries, I have been strongly impressed by an art public composed not only of the intellectual elite but also of the popular masses who attend exhibitions in large numbers. It may be that the flirtatious relationship between magic and reality, so common to life in Latin America, is all too present in a work of art. As an artist I would hope that the public, as I suspect this Latin American public does, interacts with a work of art for the reality it contains and not for its likeness with reality. When asked about the meaning of half-burnt cigarettes on the floor in many of his paintings, Fernando Botero simply replied that sometimes a painting would call for white on the bottom.

The artist, as an individual who inevitably lives within a political reality, is sometimes nationalistic. As for art, maybe it is only what artists do.

Wilfredo Chiesa
"Amore, Amore"
1985
Acrylic on canvas, 66" x 84"

QUESTIONS FROM THE AUDIENCE

Question: We have to think about what constitutes Latin American art, and what constitutes Latin American feminism. If there is no Latin American art, if there is no Latin American feminism, what do art and/or feminism have to contribute to a universal context?

Wilfredo Chiesa: Well, yes, I think there is a contribution to the universal, inasmuch as there are painters who are Latin American, who are participating in the universal activity of painting and the universal activity of feminism. Within this framework, I believe there is an absolutely direct relationship, no matter where these individuals may be found, inside or outside of Latin America.

Marta Lamas: I would agree with what Wilfredo says, but in addition I would like to say that for me things are not so unitary. Latin American feminism, seen from outside, may appear to be a unity, all of a whole, but for us who are on the inside the differences are so impressive, and so brutal, and the moments so very different. All of this has to do with the political complexion of the different countries, and also with the particular moments; or rather, a Latin American feminist who just discovered feminism last week is going to resemble a European feminist who just discovered feminism last week much more than she will resemble two old militants, European and/or Latin American, who have probably put in a lot of years already [in the feminist movement]. Let me say that, for me, to try to approach the reality from the point of a single category of whatever type seems to me very limited, whether it is one social and political phenomenon or another.

And I think that there is not a Latin American identity in the abstract sense, nor in the case of many people. There are many of us Latin Americans who in many ways, because of political circumstances, family matters and so on, feel a kinship to certain Europeans, since the whole thing is much more complicated. For me what is useful as a first category by which to approach this might be to say, well, does a Chinese literature exist? Yes, if what the Chinese write is Chinese literature; or the same for a French literature, or a literature of women, because women write it; but if someone gives me a text and doesn't tell me the nationality of the person who wrote it, I will not be able to know the identity of that person. What happens is that, in general, a person approaching a work of art or literature usually already knows who did the painting or who wrote the book, but I think really that if we are put in front of a group of paintings, I doubt very much that we would be able to detect nationality in the majority of them. There are things that are very poster-ish or pamphlet-like that allow one to say right away where they come from, but, standing in front of a work of art, I myself truthfully feel helpless to say whether the artist is European or Latin American. I feel that it pleases me or doesn't please me and that's as far as I can go.

Luis Felipe Noe: As for me, when I wrote *Antiestética* in 1965, I said that the only way to affirm the universal is by starting from the particular. I want to say also that I do not subscribe to the concept of identity, that is, identity as a general preoccupation. I believe that people naturally relate to their context in the world, which conditions them to affirm the particular; we can extract values of universal category, and thereby stand as artists of "universal" scope.

Now this matter of the conversion of an artist of universal scope

Questions from the Audience

depends also on the mechanisms of power, because those mechanisms mean that the universalization of an artist's image occurs more frequently, and is more possible, for an artist who comes from a country with power than for those who come from countries without power.

Question to Marta Lamas about what the concepts of Nationalism and Latin Americanism mean.

M.L.: Well, I am not able to talk about destiny. I can talk about concrete political interests in countries; I have seen, for example, that Chileans and Argentinians can be enemies when faced with concrete geographical questions. Or, as another example, Mexicans who live on the border with Guatemala feel more closeness to their Mayan ethnicity than with Mexican or Guatemalan nationalism. So, I believe that my concept of nationalism is not a concept that starts from anthropology. The situation in which the culture in which one lives is the only culture one knows happens rarely in Latin America. Suddenly it happens that there are people like me: I am Mexican, but the daughter of Argentinians and the granddaughter of Spaniards. So there is a mixture of nationalities, and it may be that one is not quite correct in speaking of nationalism. I believe that it is basically the culture in which one lives the first years of life that gives a frame of reference, but later the political posture and one's personal history carry a great deal of weight. In the political group in which I move, which is that of Latin American feminism, at a certain moment we were more united by an international question, of recognizing a certain common oppression in all the world of women, and then later when we began working in practical ways, we began to see the national differences.

So, I believe that nationalism is like a double-edged sword. That is, we cannot ignore all the obvious links with the fascist or Nazi question in nationalism; and on the other hand, I think that one can move about more freely if one thinks in terms conceived from a wider point of view. But I cannot speak in an objective voice; I am speaking from my point of view only.

W.C.: I feel a kinship with what Marta says. For me the question of nationalism, of identity with surroundings, is a very personal

Questions from the Audience

question. This is a question about experience based not only on the national, on the language, the culture, but also on the religion that one was brought up in, on social factors, on social classes in which one grew up... I feel myself very, very different from many Puerto Ricans, and I am sure that many Puerto Ricans find themselves feeling very different from me. But at the same time there is a common entity that is the culture, the language, the landscape, the physical surroundings in which we all grew up. I believe that, yes, there are some common Latin American denominators, the most obvious one being of course the language, but I am personally very much aware of the differences that exist between our countries. I have many, very dear Chilean friends, for example, Chile being a cold country where wine is produced. And in Puerto Rico, it's hot and we grow sugar cane. I believe that there are physical differences which translate into certain differences of identity as well.

Question: In which country do you [Marta] see more progress in feminism? And to what do you attribute this progress?

M.L.: Well, we have to see what constitutes progress. Progress in relation to the political situation in the country itself, or in the sense that there are more groups doing more things? A country like Mexico has many feminist groups, with centers, classes given at the university, and there is a great deal of information and all that, but it has little political influence. Or rather, the feminists don't count on the political structure of Mexico, nor on government actions, nor on what the left does. And in Chile, a dictatorship, the Chilean feminists have a political presence, a political role with the left and the government that we only wish we had in Mexico. And in Peru the feminists have managed to launch independent deputies; independent, let's say, in the sense that they are supported by the left, but not by the feminist movement which feels that if the feminists participate in an official political parliamentary body that that constitutes almost a betrayal of feminism; there, the movement is totally fragmented. In Argentina and Brazil there are feminist functionaries in high governmental posts, with the democratic *apertura;* and that is also questioned by the feminist movement. What will be the indicator: that there are

Questions from the Audience

feminists in political posts? Then, it would be Brazil and Argentina, countries where in this moment there are great numbers of women in high public posts. In other countries the emphasis is not on placement within the mainstream political system. The movement offers women centers, independent centers, shelters, newspapers, publications, etc. In the Dominican Republic, for example, there is a lot going on; in Mexico, also. There is a tremendous variety.

Translated by Cola Franzen.

SIGNS OF EVERYDAY LIFE

TRANSCRIPT OF REMARKS BY CARLOS CAPELAN

When reading the title "Signs of Everyday Life," we are immediately reminded of the fact that one of the first things that Homo Sapiens did was to etch symbols on their everyday tools, paint signs on their bodies and utter words that gave them strength. This means that Homo Sapiens habitually open the doors to ritual. Each day we fulfill many functions; we become hunter, gatherer, farmer, shepherd, and shaman. The shaman, that damned little word, right?

Well, I will be using that little word for a while, so I hope you will forgive me. The shaman is someone who uses the language of contact. Shamans empty and fill themselves, get in and out, call and remain silent. They are pretty strange characters. Think of Hitler, for instance. But let us think of a nicer shaman than Hitler: one in an indigenous community, located in the Peruvian highlands; the mayor, called *Curaca* in Quechua, has to make decisions. He has to decide what to plant, where to plant, and how to distribute the water; in short, very important matters, matters of importance to everyone. And so, what does he do? He with-

Transcript of Remarks

draws, looks for an isolated place in the mountains, sits down, and remains sitting there for hours. If you ask him what he is doing, he will say he is "filling himself up with the sun."
When he has a clear answer in his mind, he returns. That is what shamans do all the time. Shamans leave and come back, withdraw and come back. The shaman is nicer than Hitler and not as nice as Michael Jackson, but . . . I am trying to demystify the notion of shaman. I think that Hitler is a shaman, I think that the *Curaca* is a shaman, I think that Michael Jackson is a shaman. They are characters who put us in contact with something.

Well then, the shaman is someone who spends all his time and energy learning a technique. His work is an organized social function, like many other trades.

Now, what in the beginning was probably common to all Homo Sapiens, that is the performing of a ritual, the act of getting in contact with something, afterwards turned into a very complex language. And this in turn gave rise to a trade. These things tell us something about the language itself, about how complex it turns out to be. But they also tell us that at a given stage in the development of society, there are many members of that society who become passive. What does that mean? It means that they need a middleman in order to perform a ritual. It means that they cannot perform it on their own, they cannot get in and out of things. It means that they cannot read the signs of everyday life.

This brings something else to mind. Levi Strauss says that we have not progressed since neolithic times; there are many modern anthropologists who share his view. They say that during this period, Homo Sapiens produced a culture that satisfied our basic needs. This culture offered us a structure of protection, and allowed us to keep on being creative.

All right, let's look at another anecdote. Fairly recently it has been discovered that in the first neolithic cities, the first city-states of the neolithic period, there was a common ritual practice: each house had a room which was designed for rituals. For example, the figure of the cow, with horns as one element, was found in every house. But the external details of the ritual were different, varying with each home. From this one can infer that in each family there was at least one shaman. And this also makes me think of the ritual rooms we have in our houses nowadays, the living

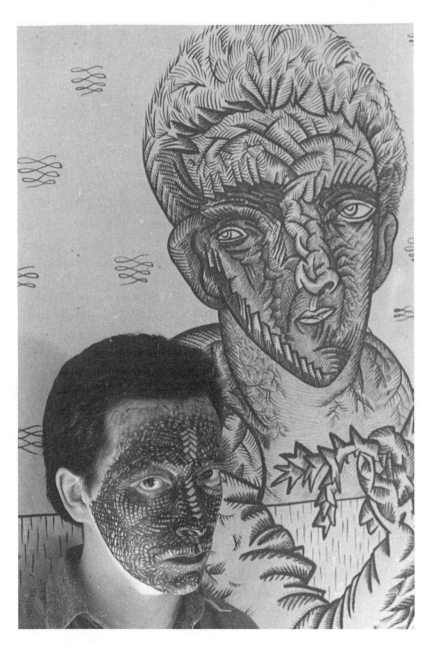

Carlos Capelan
"Dubbed Self-Portrait" from the series "The Face"
1985
Photo: Miguel Pena and Carlos Capelan

Carlos Capelan
"Rock Painting"
1985
Valdottavo-Toscany-Italy
Photo: Joseph Montague

room with the TV set for instance, our little places with little televised shrines.

The figure of the shaman, now organized at the social level, gives rise to structures that differ greatly from one another. It produces the bureaucracy of the Vatican and the Christian mystics, the Germanic clans organized around animal figures: the bear, for example, and the eagle. And it also produces the SS and the Gestapo. The figure of the shaman produces Persian poetry and psychedelic culture. And, believe it or not, shamanic experience is also behind the origin of certain schools of art, though it seems we have forgotten this fact.

Another way to look at this topic—the signs of everyday life—is through Biblical myth. Paradise, Adam and Eve, the loss of innocence and the Fall. Adam and Eve live in paradisiac relation to reality, reality is explained by itself, they are innocent; they are not ashamed of their own bodies, for instance. Then, once they commit the sin of thinking about their origin, about their bodies, they are driven out of Paradise. Two angels with flaming swords guard and block the way back. Now, what happens? The analogy with the political refugee is obvious, isn't it? Once he commits the political sin of questioning his origins and his social future, the refugee is driven into exile, right? In this case we also find angels with flaming swords, with electric prods, with machine guns and God knows what else, who guard and block the way back. Oftentimes exile can be seen as an initiation experience that completely alters our relation to everyday life. Our original relationship to things, our innocent relationship, is lost. Our neighborhood is not our neighborhood anymore, and our everyday life is dislocated. Facing exile, the first two extreme alternatives are: to deny the change of reality, which means protecting yourself, creating a ghetto, continuing to live in a bubble which links us more to the past than to the present or to the immediate; or, to rename the world, accepting another reality, creating a different dimension of everyday life.

What happens now? Here I do not want to categorize; whatever alternative the refugee chooses, both imply choosing to live an elaborated reality. Both imply that the signs of everyday life are being elaborated. It is the loss of the initial innocence, and the recreation of innocence. The inhabitant of a ghetto knows that

Transcript of Remarks

the ghetto is not something, the ghetto evokes something. The inhabitant of a ghetto knows that s/he is living an artistic, created reality. I would say that in the ghetto the reality is profoundly creative, it is re-creative.

This finally brings me to another topic which I also see as linked to all this, which is the problem of *pluriculturidad* (plural cultures). In Latin America, in México, for example, 90 indigenous languages are spoken. Not 90 indigenous dialects but 90 indigenous languages are spoken; this gives us a very special plural culture, right? Each cultural nucleus encodes reality in its own way. A plural culture offers us more opportunities for choosing alternatives, a larger range of possible answers. It also teaches us tolerance; it teaches us the meaning of tolerance. Well, this tolerance means that we are always ready to admit that we have only one version of things, and that there are other versions for these same things, and that there will always be other versions; and that these may be accepted by us. That is the enormous force that I feel in Latin America; that reality can always become a different reality. To cling to just one version of reality in Latin America is to misunderstand ourselves.

Well, the paradox is that we are millions, hundreds of millions of people living in Latin America, and that generally two languages are spoken: Spanish and Portuguese. Well, we Americans— actually, *we* are the Americans, right? Those who come from this country are the *gringos*— We Americans, oh, well, the *gringos* too, use a language which experiences exile. Our languages originate in Europe and they describe the European landscape. Then these very same languages do a very funny thing, they jump, make a circus pirouette, and start to describe a totally new landscape, which is foreign to the origins of that language. And there is a vast sea between the two realities expressed in that very same language. And on top of that I can imagine a sea with flaming swords that blocks the way to that language, because many times we cannot communicate among ourselves; when we go to Europe it is as if there were no return, through language, to Europe, right? Sometimes it is hard to get through those flaming swords.

In short, I think that, yes, there are fundamental differences between the relationship Latin Americans have with their plural culture and one the North American have with their own. But

Carlos Capelán

living in Europe I realized that Americans all have one thing in common—that Europeans see us all as Barbarians.

Well, signs of everyday life . . . .To quote an old friend of mine, a Chinese poet I have just invented, whose name is Paeng Guenk, says, "carrying water and gathering wood are two miraculous acts."

QUESTIONS FROM THE AUDIENCE

Question about the relation of the German SS to the concept of shaman.

C.C.: Yes, the internal units of the SS used to perform shamanic rites. Since time immemorial there were the bear rituals, that is the Bear Clan, in Germany. It is a ritual act in which the members perform a series of dances and chants through which they become possessed with the spirit of the bear. This ritual dates from the paleolithic period, when we were still hunters, and became, through rituals, the object of our hunting.

Many of these things have survived until today; in European cultures there are still many rites, although they are dying out more and more. This kind of ritual was practiced systematically among SS officers; it ended with orgies, most of the time with sexual connotations, and whose final objective was, as Erich Fromm says, regressive and not progressive. Fromm makes a distinction between progressive rituals, rituals which take us a step forward, and regressive rituals; the regressive ritual is where the person wants to go back to the mother, to stop the world. And the SS ritual, relative to the Bear Ritual, was not progressive in the sense of acquiring the bear's strength as a bear, but simply acquiring the brutality of the animal.

Question about why Capelán refers to Michael Jackson as a shaman.

C.C.: His whole appearance, his whole image is that of a shaman. The way he looks after his career is that of a shaman. He is predestined; he possesses all of the external attributes. He is predestined to his function, he is a chosen one, he has withdrawn, he has left. He leaves and returns to us. He breaks his exile and returns, he is in contact with forces foreign to us. I think his lover is a snake or an ape, or something like that; he lets us know that he has completely private rites. On top of that he changes his image, his appearance, he transforms himself. It is incredible, isn't it? And he really transforms himself, on stage we see him change from one video to the next, we see him changing his image, right? And then, well, the kind of answer that he gets from the audience is the usual answer, it is a ritual one.

Question from Cristina Pacheco: As for Michael Jackson, it worries me very much that you compare him with a shaman because of one thing; I am not versed on the subject and I really do not know what lies beneath the face of a shaman, but Jackson is a man who denies his own face. He constantly undergoes operations in order to look like a beautiful woman, but not like himself; and though I think that the shaman should definitely be masked, he should not brutally erase his face. So, then, he is a very special shaman. isn't he?

C.C.: Yes, definitely, he is very special, otherwise he would not be so rich. He uses the mask; the mask is a common tool of the shaman. There are masks that are used to communicate something and masks that are used to hide something. There are masks used to get in contact with something, and if I wear a bear mask, as we were saying before, I become the bear; and there is a mask which is the mask of everyday ritual, of the completely superficial ritual, that of the Venetian Carnival, like the mask to disguise myself, to turn into another person.

Question from Cristina Pacheco: But I think that, for one reason, his mask is not that superficial. The first thing that Jackson denies are his African features; he changed his nose the way someone else might wear green lenses in order to look like a Saxon. How can I respect as a shaman of my time a person who has no respect for the beauty of the Black face? I cannot accept it.

C.C.: I agree with you, but here I am not categorizing. I am not saying which shaman is the best. I have my preferences. The one

I like most is the *Curaca* from the Andes, but I cannot categorize, I am just talking about the phenomenon in a general way.

Question about whether there are female shamans.

C.C.: Yes, for sure. The first example that comes to mind are the Greek Vestal Virgins, the women chosen to get in contact with the gods. Not to mention for instance very important mystic figures like Sor Juana Inés de la Cruz, right? Besides that, everybody knows that women live more in a ritual world than men do. Well, for the male, paternity is a social fact, and is eminently social, but for the female it is a way of getting in contact with something, with natural forces, it is a way of transcending. Since the beginning, woman has generated rituals in a more natural way than man.

Question about how shamans operate in a society.

C.C.: I think that there are people who can get in contact with things, who can express the sentiment of many people, and who can find within themselves things that many people need to find. This way the person takes upon him/herself needs that other people also have. I think that Hitler, as well as Michael Jackson, adopt a shamanistic attitude towards their audience and the audience bestows on them, as figures, a shamanic value. It is important that we have an active relationship when we see a figure that has power, that is potent, that we have an active relationship to their message. And not only because a fellow has personality or energy, or because s/he has the possibility of getting in contact with something which is not accessible to the rest of us, we do not have to believe in the message. What I mean is that no matter how hard Reagan tries to give off a shamanistic attitude, I do not buy it, ok?

Translated by Soledad Gelles.

TRANSCRIPT OF REMARKS BY CRISTINA PACHECO

I want to be very honest; I am no expert in discussions of this kind, because I have no theoretical gift. And sometimes I do not have time for it. I feel that today, precisely because of all that is happening in Mexico, there is a need for more action, rather than meditation. I come from a very ancient country which lately has taken to being reborn on a daily basis. And when I say this it is not for effect, but rather I am trying to capture something which began happening a long time ago and that is now manifested clearly in everyday life.

Everyday life is the topic of my work from beginning to end. It is true, I am a journalist, but literature is not alien to me. I am not the kind of writer who is a journalist one minute, and then a writer the next, because s/he also writes books. Writers work with language, and I am a writer throughout the entire spectrum of writing. I go from newspaper writing, to weekly articles, to radio and TV copy. I do not know if that is a good or a bad way to work, but I am doing what I wanted to do and maybe because of that I do not mind being as old as I am, and I notice that I am the only one who mentioned age here, but I think it is alright. Yes, it is important for me to state how old I am because I did not betray the girl I used to be. I do not know if I am a good or a bad journalist, a good or bad writer, but I find myself with the job I wanted. And the direction I wanted to take is that of my people; that is where I belong.

For many years now, since I first started writing, the subject and voices of my work come from the vast marginal population that exists in my country. I became interested in this part of Mexico not for snobbish reasons or because it was in vogue, but because that's where I belong, 100%. My parents were peasants, who then became merchants; they later migrated to the *barrio* in Mexico City, and then they went through all those hardships which allow one to reach places like this or to have audiences like the one I have at present. What I mean is that I went from the tiny school of my home village to the school in the big city, then to the *preparatoria,* then—an enormous privilege for girls of my status at that time—to the University. Somehow, due to my indigenous and peasant origins, I suffered discrimination. It does not bother me to say that word because I think I have long since overcome it and can say it very proudly. This has allowed me to see the conditions in which a great part of the Mexican population lives—or rather survives, a better term, I think. It is a true privilege for me to have been able to leave such a situation, because one lives in a kind of tomb when one is poor, when one has no means, when one is part of an agrarian community which is totally despised, because that is unfortunately the way it is in my country. Just going to school is a great privilege.

In order for you to understand me you have to keep in mind that I am not a girl who was young in the Sixties or Seventies. I was born in 1941, and the 1950s offered few possibilities for young women in my country and in my circumstances. I explored some of them. For instance, I was a market vendor, I was a salesperson in department stores where it was forbidden to sit down, talk or turn your face anywhere but to the customer. And there were different kinds of severe oppression against women. I want to make clear that the oppression that I was subject to did not come from men—not at all, they were always excellent colleagues, excellent teachers and excellent friends—because in the

Transcript of Remarks

end the people, the men who I dealt with, were also marginalized beings, as oppressed as the women were. So from that time on I learned—I would rather say I sensed—that these movements that we see today as liberating can have no future (and I hope that I am not offending anybody) if they do not take into account the vindication and liberation of men as well, because it is also very necessary, almost as necessary as that of women, at least in Mexico.

Since I felt very privileged to be able to attend school, I thought that if somehow I could fulfill my proposed destiny, I would have to give back to my class and my people what they had offered me. So that I could go to school, my siblings did not; so that I could have a book, my siblings did not have one. And so the time arrived when I started to make my way in journalism because I had never sought any other activity, though I had those other jobs. I decided to devote myself entirely to my work, to give a voice to the men and the women who do not have one in my country, just because they belong to the marginalized class.

Curiously enough, a very special struggle with this goal began, one which, of course, cannot even be imagined today. If you go to Mexico and read the publications, newspapers, magazines or watch TV, you will see that a good number of contributors are women, and that we occupy positions that in the past were assigned only to men. When I started to work in journalism in 1963, I was already married to a poet, my husband and companion, José Emilio Pacheco. To say that I wanted to become a writer was problematic because he was already a very famous man, though he was quite young. So I took the only possible way out, which was to hide my identity from everyone, becoming a man in 1964. I became a man called Juan Angel Real, who wrote stories in a magazine for many years; because, on top of that, I did not have the credentials to write short stories. So I told the magazine's director that I wanted to give him a series of interviews, interviews that I had not actually done. They were simply things that I remembered seeing at the *rancho,* in town or in the *barrio,* very new and colorful things because no one had seen them before.

I learned to tell these stories thanks to my mother, a very talented woman who had nothing, or thought she had nothing, and died thinking she had nothing, when in fact she was a beautiful, intelligent and wonderful woman. She told us those stories in order to entertain us when we were kids. To keep us from going out in the street or asking her for something to eat, she would say, "Hold on, I'm going to tell you a story, come here." It was fantastic. Literature is useful, I learned that literature must be useful, you can eat from it too, I mean it. She would sit down and say, "You see that man sitting or standing over there?" "What about him?" "That man must be from Veracruz. See how the sunlight doesn't bother him; I'll also tell you why he is wearing that blue suit. And I'll tell you what he ate." Then she would make up for us a kind of quick scenario and immediately thereafter, it is hard to believe, she would tell us that man's story, with a Veracruz accent. Sure, it was fantastic. She was a woman who learned to write the way one should learn to write, namely by listening, and thanks to that, well I am not sure, something stayed with me, the ability to narrate. I wish I could tell stories the way she did. She is dead now but I wish you could listen to her. I wish I had her wonderful gift.

But anyway, I started being a man with a very serious problem, because this man started interviewing boxers, prostitutes, people among whom I grew up. I grew up with thieves and with . . . but it does not bother me, these people were charming and good to us. They gave us food, they lent us money on weekends, they took us to parties, they let us watch them make love. It was fantastic, it was all for free, yes, it was beautiful. Then, naturally, everybody starts to ask, who is the man who writes these weird interviews? The only ones who knew were my husband, José Emilio, and the magazine's director. But the owner did not know. The owner was the entrepreneur who promoted Buñuel's latter filmmaking career, Gustavo Alatriste; "Viridiana," "Nazarín," all those films were financed by the magazine I used to work for. And one day I wrote a tragic and terrible story, the story of one of my brothers, who had a physically abnormal child. So I wrote the story and nobody paid any attention to it because I wanted to purge myself of that terrible tale. But Buñuel saw it—Buñuel, who was coming to see Alatriste so that he would finance Silvia Pinal's films. And he said, "I want to meet this Juan Angel Real because I want to film this story." And the dilemma, well, you know the answer, was that when he saw that it was a woman he simply lost all interest, and

Transcript of Remarks

so my relationship with cinema and with Buñuel ended. Well sure, it had to be that way.

Well, I finally turned that into the center of my life and have until now been making a living out of journalism because every week I write a story about current things that happen in the city. They are things that I see, or if a picture excites and seduces me, I write a story about that picture, about a gesture, about a conversation over the phone, but it is always based on reality. A while ago, the poet you invented, your Chinese poet, said that to carry water is miraculous. I am sure there is nothing more miraculous or extraordinary than to carry water. Because I have seen it and lived it, and I am convinced that that can be the subject of literature. It is funny, but when I started to write, one had to look for great themes, women had to talk about maternity, passion; yes, all that is in there, sure it is, but it is in everyday life; there, where we carry water and throw out the garbage and knock on the door or break a glass or get into a fight. What I want to say, and what I tried to and will keep on trying to say, is to turn the most elemental material of everyday life into the essence of writing.

I would not be able to write these stories if I were not an active journalist who is totally devoted to the marginal classes, and who can go from one end to the other in México City in the very same day. And when I say from one end to the other, I mean from one century to another. I can be in the northern part of Insurgentes—the northern part of Insurgentes is the Stone Age in some places—and on the same day go to the other end and be in the 21st century, where everything is computerized, absolutely immaculate, where the water is sterilized, where you can eat mangos in December or cherries in May, it does not matter. I can also capture this world thanks to television; eight or nine years ago I started a TV series (supposed to be impossible to pull off), which simply consisted of going into the streets and capturing people's problems the way they happen. If I found you there I would ask you how a girl lives here in Boston, what the problems are that you encounter at home or with the authorities. You can imagine that in the beginning, people were scared when they saw me and they would not come out, afraid I was sent by the government. They said, this lady comes from PRI[1], to see what is going on. Little by little we gained their confidence, and nowadays they are the ones who actually call me at home and ask me to go film a problem, and there are also people who want to tell me their life stories, and then narrate them. This is a very important task, especially in the *barrios,* where there are no newspapers, where people cannot afford them.

There, someone buys a newspaper, he cuts out some stories and then posts them on the corner, and the rest read it. And believe me, I don't think this happens because my work is so good, it is probably not as good as I would like it to be. It is just that the story being told concerns all those who read it. And what has been achieved and what we want now is that in every page of a book there is the voice of people like us, people who get old, have wrinkles, are sick, suddenly have the fear that "oh, I'm 40, what should I do? I won't have plastic surgery!" Yes, that is wonderful, I want to see myself in those pages, and believe me, sometimes you need courage because this is a very tough world for a woman who lives in a fearless way.

I intend to keep on living that way. I want to die, as we Mexicans say, *en la raya.* And I want to reach my last day looking back and saying that every woman behind me, every year, all the Cristinas that are behind me, always sought out the same thing; the voice of a people which, curiously enough with this sad celebration—I am sorry but for me it is sad—of the Fifth Centenary, is starting to express itself, saying that although I am an Indian, although I am poor, although I do not speak English, although I do not have credit cards, although I do not have a fashionable car, I am a human being, and you should all listen to me. And, as I said before, this is how our country, our ancient country, is reborn every day in the voices of human beings called Pedro, or María, or Cristina, or sometimes names that we are not even able to pronounce.

QUESTIONS FROM THE AUDIENCE

Question about the term "magical realism," and the extent to which it is a useful or a confusing term.

Transcript of Remarks

C.P.: Well, I hope my answer does not bother you, but in a country where what is going on goes on, where things happen the way they do in my country now, where magic is everywhere, to talk about magical realism seems to me really impossible. I cannot talk about that. To tell the truth, I have never seen more magic than in 1985, seeing the city totally destroyed, and the people—yes, all of us—grabbing the stones and putting them in their place, because—do you know something?—we love that place which is the most polluted place in the world, and we love it in spite of that. The magic of love, the magic of the attraction to the ghastly and sordid which our city is, and to the profound and terrible, I cannot describe it otherwise, is the magic that allows us to survive there, allows the city itself to survive. You will understand that, facing this . . . no, I have no answer regarding the magical realism of literature.

Question: As for rituals and shamans and everyday life and magical realism, I would like you to tell us a bit about the México of the earthquake and about the México which produces something like the *superbarrio*.

C.P.: Although I managed to write the first book of tales about the earthquake during that time, I think I will never be able to clearly express the sensation, but above all the sound, of that moment. You cannot imagine what it was like to hear the earth. Just pretend everything was made of glass, and we were looking for something, for some place that was not broken. Everything was destroyed, it was all like some sort of bell, and we were all asking which bells were tolling, since there never used to be any. At least in my neighborhood there were none. Nonetheless it was like a deep complaint coming from the city, a complaint which we have not escaped from yet. You cannot imagine what it was like, walking days and days through the blacked-out city. It was totally destroyed, in ruins. You came to a house and said, but my friend Armando or Margarita, or whoever, used to live here; the house was not even there, neither your friends, nor anyone else.

However, among the many people I found and saw during the earthquake—because I went out immediately to try to work with TV and cameras—I found a man I will never forget. For me he is the symbol of the earthquake, even more than the dead people, more than the flattened buildings. This man was standing alone, in shirt sleeves, the very same morning of September 19. He was walking around a fallen building—actually it had sunk, because another one had fallen on top of it—and nothing was left. We knew that the people who had been there were all dead, and we knew it because of the white blankets. We were seeing how the Red Cross' stretcher bearers threw a white blanket wherever the rescuers were working, and we knew that for each white blanket there was a corpse. This man was walking here and there, tearing his hair out, and he addressed us all and said "she was naked and she is dead. She belongs to me. . .you have no reason to be here, her death belongs to me." What could I say? I knew what this man was going through, but I could not do anything but turn around and leave him. I had to respect his wish. At some point all of us, absolutely all of us, turned around and left; we left him by himself, with his dead, and with the rest of them, because in that building everyone had disappeared.

There were many scenes like this in the city. The most dramatic ones, maybe, are those we saw in the old seamstress-factories. No one knew that there were clandestine factories, and if we knew it we ignored it, out of cowardice or indifference. In these factories, which were miserable little rooms with a door but no windows, there were machines, rolls of cloth, files, safes, dollars—this fact is very important. There were some stores which refused to rescue the seamstresses. The seamstresses were in contact with us journalists because there was a telephone in the building's basement; they were saying "there is still a line, we are 24, 23, 22." They were telling us how many were left, how many had died. While we were notifying the workshops' owners—and this sounds incredible—they refused to take the corpses out because they wanted the safes and dollars first.

Many of the ruined houses allowed us to see families just like mine, families that everyone told me I had invented, that did not exist, that were a product of a sick imagination. Walls fell down and we saw families where 15 people lived in one room. Where a couple occupies a space of 2 x 2 meters, separated by a piece of cloth from another couple which in turn is separated from another, and they pay stratospheric amounts of money just to live

Transcript of Remarks

in México City. Many of these people are peasants. They go to México City and they endure these conditions, just to have *some* day—and I really mean some day—the chance to work.

Once the walls of the whole city had fallen, once the walls which divided the city were in ruins, the ghettos of rich and poor, people started to realize (those who had cars, houses, condos) that there was another México which was terrible, which was so close to them, where there was a lack of housing, where people were living in 16th century houses, with no plumbing or windows. For example I wrote a story about a woman who had never seen the light of day; she had always lived in a basement, and the only thing she saw during her life were the feet of the people who walked by. And she noticed years passing through the changing fashions. She saw her life passing by in peoples' feet. She never saw anything, she spent all her life buried there. She got out of her house because the building fell down and they did not allow her to live there anymore because she was paying too little.

What is happening to people? Well, they are being thrown out of their houses. The owners of the old lots took advantage of the fact that the houses had fallen down, to sell them for more or to ask higher prices for the houses that did not fall. People started to get organized, started to worry. They started to communicate from one neighborhood to another, asking "what are you going to do, how are you going to live, what are we going to do?"

Question about the attack on Carlos Fuentes by Enrique Krauze.

C.P.: Well, you have already seen the consequences. Who won the Nobel Prize? For many people, the consequences of that article, more than the direct or indirect polemic between Carlos Fuentes and Octavio Paz, were definitive. I, of course, have long thought that Octavio deserves the prize because he is a great poet and essayist, he is a brilliant writer. But I regret—and believe me I say this from the heart because he is a man I really love and owe a lot to—I regret that his words and their light or the brilliance of his mind are arousing the saddest part, precisely, for our countries; the right wing, and imperialism. It is truly regrettable. It is very painful, But let us not lose sight of Octavio's good side, Octavio's poetry and his immense talent as an essayist.

Cristina Pacheco

When this matter [of the Krauze polemic] was brought up in international symposia, it turned into old ladies' gossip, as we call it. They started to pull each other's hair, and one realized that behind this, Krauze wanted to play a little with Paz so that he would get the Nobel Prize at the cost of discrediting Carlos, who was a potential rival of Octavio's, and the result is that both of them were out of the game. I think that Carlos' attitude was a bit more noble and clean because he did not deign to say a single word about it, which was correct.

Question about the Mexican opposition movement in the upcoming elections.

C.P.: You are talking about Cuauhtémoc Cárdenas, aren't you? Well, I think that nowadays everything counts, yes, everything counts. Our need for change to come about is so great that we will cling to these immediate symbols. Moreover if it is a person who, I must say, is really extraordinary in one respect. I had the opportunity to interview him when he was thrown out of the PRI a year ago, when he left the party. I confess—and I have told him so—that when I went to his house I thought, "Oh my God, I am going to interview Don Lázaro's son, well, how interesting"—it is always interesting to interview Don Lázaro's son. He personally opened the door and when I saw him I thought, "I am going to interview Cuauhtémoc Cárdenas," and when I saw him smile I thought "I am going to vote for this guy when he becomes a candidate for President of the Republic." And when I heard him talk with moderation and maturity about the political problems we are living with, and above all when I saw the intelligence with which he is calming down people's desire to take up violence— because there are many anxious people who say "enough of this, whatever it takes"—he, who could have won, and who could win if he would force the situation a bit, says "No, we have to think. No situation can be good if it is founded on bloodshed, because the ones on top could easily say, "you all go revolt, let us make war, and I will wait here and when it is all over you can call me and I will start governing." No, that cannot be good. Nothing, I tell you nothing, rooted in someone else's blood, can be good." And if he can avoid it he is avoiding it, and he is doing so in a

179

brilliant way. As such he is much more than a symbol, and if this is the fifth sun, well I do not know if it will mark the end of a world but for me, and I think for all of us, it signals a beginning.

Translated by Soledad Gelles.

SIGNS OF EVERYDAY LIFE

FRANCISCO MÉNDEZ-DIEZ

Boto Grinerón Awana Luma Moropo[1]
(The body is from Cuba, the spirit from Africa)
The Caribbean, according to Gerardo Mosquera, is a time machine that combines in the same environment the rites and traditions of the so-called "primitive" people with rules of production ranging from feudalism to early capitalism.

Each individual contributes his/her racial heritage and traditions by actively participating in this historical evolution. Therefore, we find startling cases like the one of the university professor who simultaneously teaches dialectical materialism and, as a *santero*[2], practices the spiritual works so that the *orishas*[3] will assist him in his studies of Descartes.

If we find this contradictory, it's worth remembering Buñuel, who understood contradictions, and referred to Latin America as the most surrealist region of the world.

Awarandaria Warandaria Sere
(Open your eyes to know your enemy)
I am Cuban, a worker in the visual arts. My childhood during the Revolution was that period Martí referred to as "The Golden

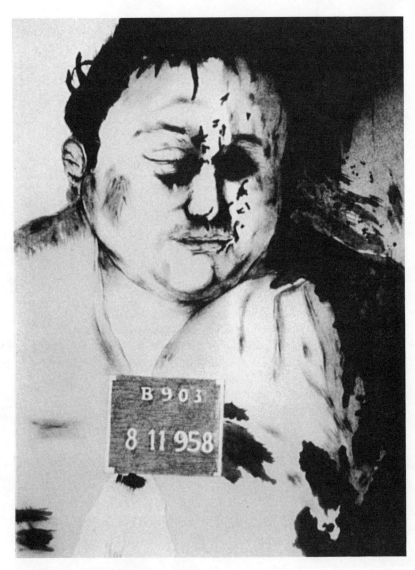

Francisco Mendez-Diez
"Chiffa"
1979
Lithograph, 22" x 30"

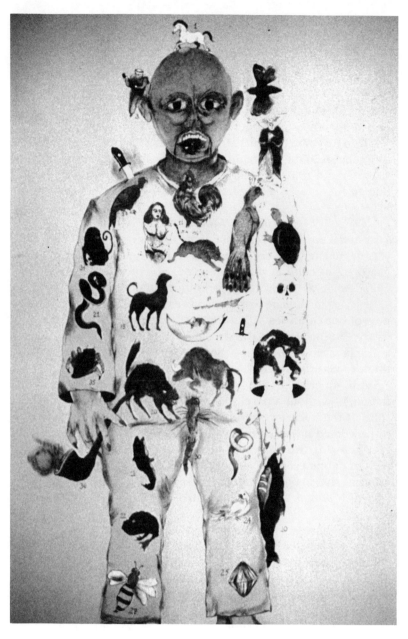

Francisco Mendez-Diez
"Salvador"
1981
Lithograph, 22" x 30"

Age." And even though I work and live in the U.S., with the implicit potential for alienation that this contradiction entails, Cuba is my culture, my people, the sign that sparks the necessary energy for my artistic endeavors.

Diego Rivera tells us that all art is propaganda and that the only difference is in the inclination of the propaganda. Rivera emphasizes art as a universal language and as an activity essential to human life—not as a privilege of the few.

Ochu Bu Odoki Enu Enyía
(It's better to fall in the river than in other people's tongues)
Unfortunately, Rivera's words have been appropriated by the guardians of culture, who refer to our arts by using slogans and clichés such as "political," "primitive" and "derivative" art.

Believers in a square world will never mention the cultural richness of our countries. It is a richness that encompasses the ability to read the signs on the sky's curvature, the ability to receive and appreciate *Tlaloc's*[4] rain, the capacity to understand *Changó's*[5] thunder and the symbols of *Chiffá*[6].

Latin America is like the *ceiba*[7] tree—sacred tree of the *lucumí*[8]—without a navel, but always growing from within. In spite of the huckster, who tries to sell us a car that won't run, or powdered milk that can make our children grow up without ever knowing their mother's breasts and who, in his arrogance, tries to define even our language . . . All of this, without understanding that in our *Yoruba* tradition there is a male *Changó* and a female *Changó,* and that both clutch the sword and quell storms.

Ochumare Oya Re Oyo
(When the rainbow appears, rain disappears)
Let me share with you a passage from our history:

> In Cubanacán, the *cacique*[9] Hatuey had finally been captured and sentenced to die at the stake.
> A distinguished priest, Bartolomé de las Casas, protector of the Indians, cannot reverse the sentence but perhaps he can save the Indian's life.
> "Hatuey, convert to Christianity and you will go to Heaven, where you'll be happy forever and after."

Hatuey responds, "And the Spaniards, do they go to Heaven?"
"Yes, of course," replies Bartolomé.
"Then burn me!"

"It is starting from poetry," José Lezama Lima reminds us, that "we exude the greatest amount of light, that a people can pour out on earth, up to now."

Asere Ebion Beromo, Ita Mariba Ndié Ekrukoro
(When the sun rises, it rises for all)

QUESTIONS FROM THE AUDIENCE

Question about the syncretization of Christian and African ritual.

F.M.-D.: When the Africans were brought to the Caribbean, they were prohibited from practicing their religions. The majority of Africans who came to Cuba were Yorubas, and because of slavery they were not allowed to express themselves, not through religion, not even through music, they were not even allowed to drum. And a way to continue practicing their religion was to use the saints of the Catholic faith, re-interpreting them or disguising their gods through them. And Changó, who is the Yoruba god of iron and thunder, turned into Santa Barbara. It is very interesting because I have read that eventually the Pope took Santa Barbara out of the Saints' Pantheon. Santa Barbara or Changó was something that was indivisible. The celebration of December 4th was referred to as "let's go celebrate Santa Barbara" or "let's dance to Changó," no matter if one was African, or Spanish, or whatever. But the belief is that there is a male and a female Changó. Usually the male is represented like Santa Barbara according to the Catholic tradition, but with a castle; when you see a statue of Santa Barbara with a castle, it is a male.

Question about the planned 1992 celebrations of Columbus' arrival in the Americas.

Signs of Everyday Life

F.M.-D.: Europe's transformation results from the discovery of America. Europe grows when America is discovered. I think that we contributed quite a lot to that, I mean to those who believed that the world was square. If in this celebration one could include all that happened during the so-called discovery of America, and if we would involve ourselves in the process of learning the exact nature of our discovery and colonization, including the political situation, the *encomienda,* the exploitation and slavery of the Indians, then it would be a celebration of all American races and cultures; that would be wonderful.

Question about the politicization of art.

F.M.-D.: I think that if someone tells you that the content of art is not political, he is always lying. Abstract art, even abstract expressionism, has political ramifications, political roots. Many of the artists who stood out in that movement were European immigrants. And if you think of the historical context, you realize that there could be no reality, no one wanted to face reality in this country then. We are accused of having a politicized art, they say our art is very political—since you are a Latin American, your art is political—and that is forbidden, art must not be politicized, only aesthetic. And what about Goya? It is just another way of oppressing us.

Question continues about the social power of art.

F.M.-D.: But art can contribute, and it can help. For instance we have the case of Perú with *Sendero Luminoso,* the "Shining Path," and it is true that works of art will not change the situation nor help *Sendero,* but we have Abimael Guzmán, *Sendero Luminoso's* apparent leader, its founder, and much of what we know about Abimael Guzmán's image comes to us through the popular arts. It comes from posters, graffitti, pamphlets, poems and songs; to such an extent that in Perú it is forbidden to represent or mention Abimael Guzmán's name. Somehow the government is afraid of these popular arts, which try to fill the streets with Abimael Guzmán's image.

Question about Méndez-Diez' work on mural projects, which

involve groups of children, and about the politicization of those children through the process of painting the murals.

F.M.-D.: One of the first things the Spaniards did during the Conquest was to destroy the monuments, idols and cities; and if we think about the artistic quality of the stone engravings, and of the cities, the first thing they did was to destroy, to tear down all those stones, as a way to start destroying the people. The issue is not that, in doing art, we will elect Michael Dukakis instead of Ronald Reagan, but definitely—well, George Bush is the same thing—we can definitely influence and develop the spirit of our people.

Comment from Cristina Pacheco: In relation to what you are saying, it is true that the Spaniards wanted to destroy every remnant of indigenous art, but nowadays, in these moments when Mexico is changing in such a significant way, something very important has happened in the domain of pre-Hispanic art. In the building of the old *Arzobispado,* in Moneda number 4, they were trying to lift a fountain because this fountain had started to sink—believe it or not this all happened recently, it is part of Mexican surrealism. When they started to repair the fountain, the archaeologists in charge (because the fountain dates from the 18th century) began to sink down and down, and they found the most beautiful stone of all the ones we have found so far. This stone has a diameter of 2.7 meters, and in its center has a number of engravings around it. It is perhaps more beautiful than the *Coyolxauqui,* as beautiful as the Aztec Calendar. In its center it has a terrible face, a dreadful face, one can see it sticking out: it is a mask with an open mouth. In this mask there was a ring, to which the warrior's waist was tied. Whatever happened, the warrior was going to die a fantastic death, very similar to the one that Mexican Indians have nowadays. This warrior was allowed to fight against his foes only within this diameter, within the space covered by the stone's diameter. And he was armed with a feather, not with a real weapon, whereas the four men outside were armed with obsidians and carved bones to flay him. The warrior had to resist, and if he was a very good warrior and succeeded in resisting all the punishment inflicted by these four priests, the last one came in the end, to take and beat him—because he had the name and word

Signs of Everyday Life

of god, god's weapon—and take out his heart. And in this open mouth we see today, which is so beautiful—I hope you get to see it when you go to Mexico—they placed the still-beating heart of the Mexican. And this has been discovered today, this has come to light in these days of terrible change in the city. I think that something, something really important, is going on, precisely now that the Fifth Centenary is approaching. This seems to me an important voice coming from the past.

Translated by Cristina Cardalda.

Francisco Mendez-Diez
"Havana, B.C."
1980
Lithograph, 22" x 30"

LATIN AMERICA
IN NORTH AMERICA

TRANSCRIPT OF REMARKS BY GERARDO MOSQUERA

Well, my presentation will be very modest. I simply wish to offer for discussion a few ideas from the opposite point of view, by making reference to the North American influence in Latin America. Obviously, in this case it is not a matter of cultural contact that comes about as a result of immigration. The North American presence and influence in Latin America is due above all to the working of the great cultural networks of movies, television, publications and museums, all of which exercise an extraordinarily strong pull on the culture of my continent. I think that it is always proper to remember that this cultural pressure is obviously based on a system of economic, political and social neo-colonialism exercised over Latin America by its powerful neighbor to the north.

An obvious point of this influence is in sports. Rather than referring to "Latin America," I like to call this region the "Baseball Zone." I mean a zone that includes Central America, the Antilles, and the northern part of South America. And since we are talking about the Border, I've had the opportunity of being present at the frontier of that baseball zone. It was in the Venezuelan

Transcript of Remarks

Andes, in one of those semi-arid areas, more than 3,000 meters high, where I watched a baseball game, complete with all the rules and regulations. It was quite a shock to me. The players were, well, very Andean-looking individuals, and it turned out to be somewhat shocking to me to see them pitching and calling strikes way up there.

In the case of my country in particular, in Cuba, well, North American influence was stronger than anywhere else except Puerto Rico. North American influence was so strong that we were even losing the Spanish language, but that was cut short by the Revolution in '59. However I give you this example of baseball because it makes a clear point with respect to another aspect of the problem, and that is that now this particular cultural influence has become internalized in many cases. Baseball may be a very simple example of this internalization, but it is a very eloquent one. I remember, for example, Fidel Castro himself talking, explaining once how he had a high-ranking official Soviet delegation visiting and there was a baseball game the very same night with a U.S. team. So, he had to see the Soviet delegation but he also wanted to see the baseball game, of course. So it occurred to him to invite the Soviets to the ball game. But since he was the host and had to be courteous, he was obliged to try to explain the rules of the game to the Russians. And then he said to them that only in that moment had he realized how complicated the game was, because he was trying to explain to the Russians that, well, a foul counted as a strike, but when there are two strikes on the batter then the foul means nothing. And then all the plays, the moves of the pitcher, the squeeze play, etc. It was impossible; he simply gave up. And I believe that this illustrates how cultural influences are sometimes internalized and come out as a result of a very deep process, and I think we have to reckon with that fact.

The stance of Latin America *vis-a-vis* that strong North American cultural influence is always that of defense of its own cultural identity. But the danger of this defense is that some take a position of total rejection. That seems to me to be the political attitude of an ostrich, one more manifestation of cultural colonialism. And on the other hand, the opposite attitude can sometimes be found, among those who submit and aspire to be simply second-hand North Americans, from south of the Rio Grande, giving up their will above all.

Valuable elements can be found in all cultures, things that can be useful to everybody. My personal point of view, as a critic confronting the great force of penetration of the powerful cultural networks surrounding us, is that one very useful tactic that some artists whom I support have adopted is to try to appropriate whatever suits us very well, whatever can be useful to us for our own culture. I refer to an active appropriation, an appropriation in our favor of what can be useful to us. Actually, this has been done frequently throughout the process of formation of Latin American culture, because of its character of synthesis. And we Latin Americans know that we make out quite well with this tactical trick. Fernando Ortiz, a Cuban anthropologist of the Malinowski school, coined a term that is quite popularly used now—instead of "acculturate," typical of the Malinowski school, he proposed "transculturate," which means that in this process in which a dominant culture tries to despoil another, a reciprocal influence may be at play that results in a product that would be a *tertium quid*, a third entity, a different one. In this regard, Latin American culture gives us some truly spectacular examples. We have only to mention the case of Jorge Luis Borges, or a Cuban writer who is less well-known in English-speaking countries, José Lezama Lima. We even find in the Afro-Cuban rites, for instance, and in a very delightful way, the existence of a very strange example of a borrowing from North American culture that has to do with spiritualism. This element of transculturation appears embodied in an Indian, but a Hollywood Indian, an Indian who even speaks through the medium in a kind of broken Spanish when the spirits come, as though he were an Indian from a Hollywood Western movie. Latin Americans use kitsch objects to represent this Indian of the Great Plains, a typical Indian of the Lakota or Sioux tribes, rather than an Indian from the Central or Southern region of the Americas. In this case we can speak of inadequate appropriation. And I think that we Latin Americans are true masters at inadequate appropriation, that is, of taking things that are off the mark and recycling them, working with them as a base.

Regarding this inadequate appropriation, I would like to read you a quote from Boris Bernstein: "The reception of external influences means the inclusion of such influences in the system of relationships of the given cultural unity, in which the received phenomena inevitably take on new meanings, and at the same time, like every innovation, restructure in some way the system received. That does not mean at all that the foreign experience was correctly assimilated, organically. On the contrary it can be borrowed externally without any understanding of its place and meaning in the other cultural system and receive a meaning that is absolutely different in the context of the receiving culture. Nevertheless the transplant was made, and a new situation created. The net of relationships that had existed until then was restructured, and had an influence on the perspective of development."

I very much like the way that Bernstein has phrased this idea, and it refers back strongly to the experience described here tonight as to the contrary situation in Latin America that I have sketched briefly. As a further comment on this type of dialectic of defense of identity—the rejection of the foreign influence at the same time that the presence of North American cultural elements are being assimilated south of the Rio Grande—it would perhaps be interesting to end with another baseball story.

It concerns the early days of the Revolution in Cuba when, as part of the opposition to the North American penetration, it was decided to Spanish-ize all the baseball language, and a hit, for instance, became an "incogible," (an "uncatchable"); a homerun was turned into "four bases," and the shortstop, nobody knows why, they called the "cemerero." Naturally, for the balk there was no possible translation, and in fact, after a couple of years of struggling with all of this, the poor TV sportscasters were going crazy and a great confusion resulted. What happened was that the hit continued to be called hit, the strike was still called "estréi," homerun kept being called "jonrón" and they just kept on pronouncing the terms as though they were Spanish, because they had by then become internalized and it was phony to try to change them. I think some of the best "jonroneros" and "cátchers" would be, for example, García Márquez or Juan Rulfo, who simply grabbed William Faulkner and Hemingway and did what they pleased with them, took advantage of every opening offered by those writers and others to enter into—to delve deeper into—the Latin American world in a very organic way. It seems to me that this open character, this character of grabbing on all sides is at the bottom of the richness of Latin American culture itself.

Finally, since I believe I have a minute left, I would like to say with respect to these problems in general, my personal position is the following: if it is true that a tendency toward the creation of a universal culture exists, we will find ourselves obliged to keep in step with it because that seems to be the tendency. The problem is to avoid what is happening now, namely that the universal culture is being fabricated on the island of Manhattan. We should strive for a universal culture to which all peoples of the world would truly contribute, each bringing something useful for all. And at the same time the process would not be a homogenization that finishes off local cultural riches. I think Coca-Cola is very good, but that doesn't mean we have to give up wine, and I think McDonald's is not all bad, but that doesn't mean we have to lose our tacos, quesadillas and arepas.

Translated by Cola Franzen.

BORDER BRUJO

GUILLERMO GOMEZ-PENA

(a performance poem from the series "Documented/Undocumented")[1]
San Diego/Tijuana 1989

"I dedicate this piece to my son Guillermo Emiliano, hoping that when he grows up, most of these words will be outdated and unnecessary."

PREFACE:

Border Brujo is a ritual, linguistic and performative journey across the US-México border.

Border Brujo first crossed the border in costume in June of 1988.

Border Brujo unfolds into 15 different personas, each speaking a different border language. And the relationship between these personas is symbolic of the one between North and South; Anglo and Latin America; myth and social reality; legality and illegality; performance art and life.

The structure is disnarrative and modular, like the border experience.

It fuses postmodern techniques with popular voices and dialectical forms borrowed from a dozen sources, such as media, tourism, pop culture, Pachuco and pinto slang and political jargon. These voices are intertwined with metacommentary and epic poetry. The epic tone reflects the epic experience of contemporary Mexican Americans.

Border Brujo speaks in Spanish to Mexicans, in Spanglish to Chicanos, in English to Anglo Americans and in tongues to other brujos and border crossers. Only the perfectly bicultural can be in complicity with him.

Border Brujo exorcises with the word the demons of the dominant cultures of both countries.

Border Brujo articulates fear, desire, trauma, sublimation, anger and misplacement.

Border Brujo suffers in his own flesh the pain of his ruptured community.

Border Brujo puts a mirror between the two countries and then breaks it in front of the audience.

Border Brujo loves and hates his audience; loves and hates himself.

Border Brujo creates a sacred space to reflect on the painful relationship between self and other. He dances between self and other. He becomes self and other, with himself.

Border Brujo negotiates several artistic traditions, including performance art, Chicano theatre, ritual theatre, border poetry and Latin American literature.

Border Brujo is a character, but he is also an alternative chronicler of life in a community.

Border Brujo is a performance artist, but he is also a cultural prisoner, a refugee, a migrant poet, a homeless shaman, and the village fool.

His performance language has no artifice whatsoever. His sole instruments consist of an altar jacket, a hat, a wig, a table, a ghetto blaster and a megaphone. There's no backstage magic.

Border Brujo practices the aesthetics of poverty and the culture of recycling so characteristic of Latin America.

Border Brujo performs distinctly inside and outside the artworld. He has appeared in galleries and theatre festivals, and also at youth centers, migrant worker centers, high schools, community events, political rallies and performance pilgrimmages.

Border Brujo is another strategy to let you know we are here

Border Brujo

to stay, and we'd better begin developing a pact of mutual cultural understanding.

> Gómez-Peña
> desde la herida infectada
> toward 1992.

COSTUMES: *altar jacket, pachuco hat, wig, dark glasses, banana necklace.*

PROPS: *portable altar, megaphone, cassette recorder, tequila bottle, toy violin, knife, syringe, shampoo bottle, etc. The props lie on a table. A digital billboard announces "SPONSORED BY TURISMO FRONTERIZO." On the back wall a pinta reads "Border Brujo (2000 BC-1989)."*

Music plays as audience enters space. A collage of Tambora, German punk, bilingual songs from Los Tigres del Norte and rap opera.

INTRODUCTION
[Soundtrack: Tarahumara violins. Border Brujo organizes his altar table, while speaking in an Indian dialect. When he is done fixing the altar he grabs megaphone and switches to English.]

dear audience
feel at home
this continent is your home
grab a cigarette
this is a smoking world
kick back
grab the crotch of your neighbor
& allow me the privilege
of reorganizing your thoughts
dear foreign audience
it's January 1st, 1847
& the U.S. hasn't invaded Mexico yet

this is Mexico *carnales!*
there is no border
we are merely divided
by the imprecision of your memory

> *[He enters into a trance & begins speaking in tongues.
> Then he switches to the voice of a drunk.]*

hey, would you just leave me alone?
just leave me alone. . .
you're just a border-crosser
a "wetback" with amnesia
who the hell invited your ancestors
to this country by the way?

I

[With eyes closed & in an epiphanic voice]

I came following your dream
& your dream became my nightmare
once here,
I dreamt you didn't exist
I dreamt a map without borders
where the Latin American archipelago
reached all the way
to the *nuyorrican* barrios of Boston and Manhattan
all the way to the pockets
of Central American refugees
in Alberta & British Columbia

[He opens his eyes]

& when I dream like this
you suffer
my dream becomes your nightmare
& pot, your only consolation

Border Brujo

II

[Sounds of rooster, the soundtrack: danzon "Imposible" by Los Hochimilcas. Voice of a Mexican soap opera actor; parts in Spanish are mispronounced.]

today, the sun came out in English
the world spins around *en inglés*
& life is just a melancholic tune
in a foreign tongue...
like this one

[He shows his tongue to the audience]

ay México
Rrrrrooommantic México
"Amigou Country"
para el gringo desvelado
Tijuana Caliente, la "O"
Mexicali Rose
para el gabacho deshauciado
El Pasou y Juarrézz
ciudades para encontrar el amor
amor que nunca existió
ay México
rrrrooommantic México
paraíso en fragmentación
mariachis desempleados
concheros desnutridos
bandidous alegris
beautiful *señoritas*
mafioso politicians
federalis que bailan el mambou
el rónchero, la cumbía, la zambía
en-tropical skyline sprayed on the wall
"dare to cross the Tequila border"
dare to cross "the line" without your coppertone
transcorporate breeze sponsored by *Turismo*
maquiladora power for the business *macho*
crunchy *nachous* to appease the hunger

[He turns into a transvestite.]

Tostadas Supreme para aliviar las penas
enchiladas y MacFa-ji-tas
mmmnn... peso little-eat so *grandi!*
where else but in México

III
*[He manipulates objects from the altar table,
speaks in a normal voice]*

*vivir y crear en California
es un tormento privilegiado
vivir en los 80s
esperar a la muerte total
ser bilingüe, bihemisférico
macizo, sereno, proto-histórico
ininteligible luego experi-mental
e incompatible con usted
sr.* Monocromatic
víctima del melting plot

[He turns into a México City ñero]

*pinto mi raya
salto la tuya
me dicen el Borges de Caléxico
el Octavio Pus de San Isidro
hablo en español, dígolo intento
y los gabachos me escuchan con recelo
(unos me interrogan con las uñas
otros me filman en Super-8)

soy posmoderno... ¿pos qué?
conceptual... ¿con qué?
experi-mental... pos qué experi-mentira
mentírame sobre tu pin-che-es-pa-ci-o-cu-pa-do*

[He does sound poem based on Mexican street voices.]

Border Brujo

IV
[He begins walking in circles and howling like a wolf, keeping a rhythm with his feet.]

crísis
craises
the biting crises
the barking crises

[He barks]

la crísis es un perro
que nos ladra desde el norte
la crísis es un Chrysler le Baron con 4 puertas

[He barks more]

soy hijo de la crísis fronteriza
soy hijo de la bruja hermafrodita
producto de una cultural cesarean
punkraca heavy-mierda all the way
el chuco funkahuátl desertor de 2 paises
rayo tardío de la corriente democratik
vengo del sur
el único de 10 que se pintó

[He turns into a merolico.]

nací entre épocas y culturas y viceversa
nací de una herida infectada
herida en llamas
herida que auuuuuulla

[He howls]

I'm a child of border crisis
a product of a cultural cesaraen
I was born between epochs & cultures
born from an infected wound

a howling wound
a flaming wound
for I am part of a new mankind
the 4th World, the migrant kind
los transterrados y descoyuntados
los que partímos y núnca llegamos
y aquí estamos aún
desempleados e incontenibles
en proceso, en ascenso, en transición
per omnia saecula saeculorum
"INVIERTA EN MEXICO"
bienes y raíces
vienes y te vas
púdrete a gusto en los United
estate still *si no te chingan*

[He continues with a sound poem.]

V
[With thick Mexican accent, pointing at specific audience members.]

I speak Spanish therefore you hate me
I speak in English therefore they hate me
I speak Spanglish therefore she speaks *ingleñol*
I speak in tongues therefore you desire me
I speak to you therefore you kill me
I speak therefore you change
I speak in English therefore you listen
I speak in English therefore I hate you
pero cuando hablo en español te adoro
but when I speak Spanish I adore you

ahora, why *carajos* do I speak Spanish?
political praxis *craneal*
I mean...
I mean...

Border Brujo

VI

[Soundtrack: Supercombo. He delivers text in the fast style of a Tijuana barker.]

welcome to the Casa de Cambio
foreign currency exchange
the Temple of Instant Transformation
the place where Tijuana y San Diego se entrepiernan
where the Third becomes the First
and the fist becomes the sphincter
here, we produce every imaginable change
money exchange *kasse*
cambio genético verbal
cambio de dólar y de nombre
cambio de esposa y oficio
de poeta a profeta
de actor a pelotari
de narco a funcionario
de mal en peor
sin cover charge
here, everything can take place
for a very reasonable fee
anything can change into something else
Mexicanos can become Chicanos
overnite
Chicanos become Hispanics
Anglo Saxons become Sandinistas
& surfers turn into soldiers of fortune
here, fanatic Catholics become swingers
& evangelists go zen
at the clap of my fingers
for a very modest amount
I can turn your *pesos* into dollars
your "coke" into flour
your dreams into nightmares
your penis into a clitoris
you name it Califa
if your name is Guillermo Gómez-Peña
I can turn it into Guermo Comes Penis

or Bill "the multi-media beaner"
or even better, *Indocumentado #00281431*
because here Spanish becomes English *ipso facto*
& life becomes art with the same speed
that *mambo* becomes jazz
tostadas become pizza
machos become transvestites
& *brujos* become performance artists
it's fun, it's fast
it's easy, it's worthwhile
you just gotta cross the border

[He stands up & performs a biblical gesture.]

Lázaro gabacho wake up and cross!!
crossss/cruzzzzz/crasssss

VII
[He begins the following text with a psalm in Latin.
He delivers text like a Catholic chant.]

Cyber-Bwana
Tezcatlipoca Electronic
Fabricante de la Imágen Internacional
Padrastro de la Incertidumbre Mundial
Legislador de la Tercera y Ultima Realidad
Gran Mano que todo lo acorrala
you ordered us to come
via TV via rock & roll
Imevisión here we are
SPANISH INTERNATIONAL NETWORK
& we are here...
to stay

[He continues with norteño accent.]

Cyber-Bwana
we are your product in a way
we are what you can only dream about

we hold the tiny artery
which links you to the past
the umbilical cord that goes back to the origins
from Homo Punk to Homo Pre-Hispanic
from high-tech to Aztec without missing a beat
without us you would go mad
without us you would forget who you really are
without us you are just another tourist lost in Puerto Vallarta

[He grabs megaphone.]

we perform, we scold you, we remind you
'cause we are so little
so fuckin' minute
what else can we do?

VIII
[Soundtrack: Tambora Sinaloense. He speaks like a drunk.]

...& you think we have nothing in common?
well, well
you are a victim of your government
& so am I...of yours
I am here 'cause your government
went down there
to my country
without a formal invitation
& took all our resources
so I came to look for them
just to look for them
nothing else

[He drinks from a bottle of shampoo.]

if you see a refugee tonight
treat him well
he's just seeking his stolen resources
if you happen to meet a migrant worker
treat him well

he's merely picking the food
that was stolen from his garden

    [He begins to scream.]

has anyone seen my stolen resources?
has anyone seen my coffee,
my copper, my banana, my gas,
my cocaine, my wrestling mask?
my my ma-ma, ma-ma-cita...mamita!!

     [He cries]

      IX
  [He speaks through the megaphone]

dear Californian
we harvest your food
we cook it
& serve it to you
we sing for you
we fix your car
we paint your house
we trim your garden
we babysit your children
& now
we even tell you what to do:
go South *Califa*
abandon your dream
& join the continental project

dear Californian,
your hours are counted
by the fingers of your unwillingness
to become part of the world
you must be scared shitless of the future

    [He speaks in tongues]

Border Brujo

I've got the future in my throat

      [He speaks in tongues]

take me or kill me *Pochtlani*
look South or go mad
I mean it *vato*

      [He speaks in tongues]

...& you dare to ask me
where have I been
all these years?

X
[He continues to speak through the megaphone.]

estimado compañero
del otro lado del espejo
there's really no danger tonight
estoy completamente desarmado
the only real danger lies
in your inability to understand me
in your unwillingness to trust
the only real danger is in your fingers
your thumb lies on the button
your index finger on the trigger
you have the weapons *maestro*
I merely have the word
my tongue is licking your wounds
it hurts but it makes sense
it's up to you to dialogue
it's up to you to dialogue

XI
[Soundtrack: Ry Cooder. He speaks like a smooth-talker,
kisses audience with a smooth-talker style.]

smack! smack!

hey, baby... baby, *güerita*
duraznito en almíbar, nalguita descolorida...
It's me, the Mexican beast
we are here to talk, to change, to ex-change
to ex-change images and fluids
to look at each other's eyes
to look at each other's mmmhhj
so let's pull down the zipper of our fears
& begin the... Binational Summit *mi vida*
but remember,
I'm not your tourist guide across the undetermined otherness
this ain't no tropical safari to *Palenke* or *Martinique*
much less a private seminar on interracial relations

[He changes to normal voice.]

this is a basic survival proposal
from a fellow Mex-american
in the debris of continental culture
& all this blood is real
the hoopla is false but the blood is real
come taste it *mi amor*

[He grabs the megaphone.]

subtext:
dear border lover
Eurídice Anglosajona
the state of interracial communication
has been seriously damaged by the AIDS crisis
we are no longer fucking our brains out
no longer masturbating across the fence
no longer exchanging binational fluids
we are merely stalking & waiting
waiting for better times
& more efficient medication
we are horny & scared
very horny & very scared
tonight we must look for other strategies

Border Brujo

& place additional importance on the word
I love you *querida amante extranjera*
but this time you have to be content with my words
la palabra alivia las heridas de la historia

XII
[He speaks in broken English.]

no, I did not qualify
my ex-landlord didn't recognize me when I called
my employers said they'd never seen me before
those art lords didn't want to sign the form
"there's no recognizable form in your art"—they said
"there's no recognizable form for your fear"—I told them
"your aggressiveness is an expression of cultural weakness"—
they replied
"but which is the form of my dignity?"—I asked rhetorically

[Pause.]

they were shocked by how articulate I was

[Voice becomes softer.]

form, form
form without content
love without saliva
art without ideas
tacos without *salsa*
life without redemption
form, form, form

[Voice changes to stylized Pachuco.]

form a coalition *carnal*
no te duermas Samurai
get a computer *pirata*
but *buzo*
if your umbilical cord breaks

there's nothing we can do
you're gone
lost in the all-encompassing fog
of the United States of America
& then,
you *es-tass jou-didou
comprehendi?*

[He continues in a normal voice.]

the day I was born
September 23 of 1955
eternity died
& the border wound became infected

the day my father died
February 17 of 1989
my last tentacle with México broke
¿ I finally became a Chicano

XIII
[He holds bottle & delivers commercial as Latino transvestite.]

Tequila Guero. . .with menthol
the new breath of old México
for the contemporary warrior
who doesn't want to give up
his language, his identity or his. . .mmhhjj
   *[He then proceeds to announce a shampoo bottle in
         an Indian dialect.]*

XIV
*[Soundtrack: "La Negra" fading in & out. He speaks like a trans-
      vestite, and clearly experiences a lot of pain.]*

ay!
ayy!!
aayyy!!!
las leyes que emasculan

Border Brujo

la orden mortal en forma de cupón
de imágen televisiva
....trémula voz eléctrica
al otro lado del teléfono
0095-619
al otro lado del other side

[He grabs the megaphone, speaks with overdone Mexican accent.]

hellou, hellou
alo Jack
can you hearr me?
can you rreally hear me?
I am finally speakin' English
...no, no, you are not to blame for the invasion of Grenada...
the air-raid to Libya wasn't your fault...
the Iran-Contra aid wasn't really your initiative
nor were the last economic sanctions to México

[Pause]

Jack, ou have delusions of grandeur
you were merely receiving instructions
...& please forgive my bad English
I came too old to this country
& I haven't been domesticated yet

[He puts down the megaphone & addresses the audience with real voice.]

the marine stood up
kicked the table
spit at my face
"you goddamn terrorist wetback!!"
& began to cry like a *chihuahua*

[Pause.]

...but the *mariachis* never stopped playing

they are still playing right now
what beautiful paradox
California sinks
& the *mariachis* keep playing
can you hear them?
can you hear them?

XV
[He speaks through the megaphone.]

hello, this is authentic Latino performance art
zero bullshit/ lots of style

*[He puts on shaman wig, delivers text with a
breathy drunken voice.]*

I am 33, the age of Christ
& this is the year of Armageddon
the "Year of the Yellow Spider"
according to Tasaday
& the Chinese "Year of the Snake"
digo la neta es que
your president & bunch have brought
sadness, radioactivity & death
to the whole damn world

[He burps & coughs.]

they've killed thousands of people
down south & overseas
& you are also responsible
como dice Chomsky
"we are all responsible
for the crimes of our governments..."
but...
you are particularly responsible
for the crimes of the CIA, the FBI,
the Border Patrol, the *Contras*...
you are responsible for all civilian mercenaries

Border Brujo

engaged in foreign causes
both military & artistic
you are also responsible for...

> *[Pause]*

why are you responsible?

[He answers in an Indian dialect, then continues as hipster.]

hey, I grow the pot...& you smoke it
I need dollars, you need magic
a perfect transaction I'd say
we both need to overcome
our particular devaluations, *que no?*

> XVI
> *[Soundtrack: Gregorian chants. He delivers text as a TV evangelist.]*

you can leave this space if you wish
there's really nowhere else to go
your house has been culturally occupied
your mind is already invaded
trust me
let's begin to talk
let's stop performing
this is an art of emergency
there's nowhere else to go
the South is in flames
the border is cancelled
& the North is occupied
by Reagan's conceptual battalion

I'm sorry for being so direct
but we are running out of time, pesos & faith
but we are running out of time, pesos & faith

XVII
[Very fast Cantinflas-like voice.]

they say I talk to gringos
they say I wasn't born in East L.A.
they say I left the Committee by choice
they say I promote "negative stereotypes" of my people
they say I sound like Pablo Neruda gone punk
they say my art is a declaration against the Holy Virgin of
    Mexican (aesthetics)
they say my politics are endangering the party
they say I'm sleeping with a post-structuralist feminist
    troublemaker
they say I have to stop riding my experimental donkey
& put my feet on the ground
once & for all
but let me tell you something
I feel no ground under my feet
I'm floating, floating
on the ether
of the present tense
of California
& the past tense
of Mexico

[He speaks in tongues.]

XVIII
[He speaks in a normal voice.]

...*porque sufro la gran ruptura*
fractura parietal en 5º grado
estar dos unidos es pura ilusión
...*porque sufro el gran destierro*
la vida es un lento destierro
good-bye *compadre transhumante*
Ulises ranchero
te apañó la migra por 9ª ocasión

Border Brujo

te quedaste sin cruzar
sin cruisin' *no hay* redemption
somos nadie en el éter desunidos
en USA desunidos
mita y míto
partidos por la mitad

[He grabs knife, gestures as though wanting to commit hara-kiri.
Speaks like a macuarro.]

soy carne de cañón
papel de hoguera
ardo en las llamas del arte contemporáneo
arde el inglés en mi garganta
arde el D.F. en mi memoria
arde la llama del movimiento
apenas
apenas
apenitas

          [He stabs himself.]

aaaaaaggggggghhhhhhhh

          [He continues with normal voice.]

& as I was crossing the border check point
this somewhat intelligent *migra*
confiscated a copy of this text
he read a few pages
& asked if I was a member
of the *Partido Chicano-Cardenista*
"*no, señor,*" I replied
"I am a member of the Tribe of the Inflamed Eyelids"
he tore my passport in half
& I proceeded to kick him in the balls
for the sake of experimentation

XIX
[Soundtrack: cumbia. He speaks like a Tijuana street hustler.]

hey mister... mixter
& you thought Mexico was South America?
you thought Castillian Spanish was better than Mexican
you thought salsa was Mexican music
you thought all Mexicans were dark-skinned & short &
  talkative like me
you thought Mexican art was a bunch of candy skulls &
  velvet paintings
you thought Mexico represented your past
& now you're realizing Mexico is your future
you thought there was a border between the 1st & 3rd world
& now you're realizing you're part of the 3rd world
& your children are hanging out with us
& your children & us are plotting against you
hey mister, eeeh mister... mister
& suddenly you woke up
& it was too late to call the priest, the cops or the
  psychiatrist
a qué pinche sustote te pegaste
y en español

XX
[He grabs the megaphone.]

hello, this is the uncensored voice of the "Latino boom":
I mean to ask you some questions
dear editor
dear curator
dear collector
dear candidate
dear anthropologist
where can we draw the line between curiosity &
  exploitation?
between dialogue & entertainment?
between democratic participation & tokenism?
where is the borderline

Border Brujo

between my Spanish & your English?
ce n'est pas ici
between my sperm & your mouth
there is a cultural void
between my wings & your knife
there's uncontrollable panic
between my words & your ears
there are 33 years of rain
& between my art & yours
there's 10,000 miles of misunderstanding

> *[He subvocalizes, then speaks in an Indian dialect,
> then continues text with a nonchalant attitude.]*

what I think is avant-garde, you think is passé
what I think is cool, you think is corny
what I think is funny, you think is cruel
what I think is fascism, you think is just life
what I think is life, you think is romantic
what I think is true, you think is literature
what I think is art, you just have no time for it
what I think is West, you think is South
what I think is America, you think is your country

> *[He stands up & screams.]*

we are so far away from one another
we are so far away from one another!!

> *[He mouths as if screaming, then continues text
> in cool style.]*

I speak therefore you misinterpret me
I am in Tijuana, you are in . . . .
I exist therefore you misunderstand me
I walk back into Spanish
for there are many concepts to protect
good-bye *compita*
extranjero en tu propio país

chao, chaocito, adieu
aufwiedersehen, caput, puut'íssimus. . . . . .

*[He performs "offensive" sign language from México.
Lights fade out.]*

-10 MINUTE INTERMISSION-

PART TWO

XXI

*[He chants text in the style of a merolico.
Soundtrack: bullfight music.]*

so, ¿a qué vienes extranjero?
¿a experimentar "peligro cultural?"
¿a tocarle los pies al brujo?
¿a pedirle perdón?
¿a ver si te reorienta hacia el poniente?
pero sus palabras te confunden aún más
te hieren, te desconsuelan
you can't even understand the guy
'cause he speaks in a foreign tongue
seems real angry & ungrateful
& you begin to wonder

*[He begins to mumble like a "red neck,"
mispronounces Spanish.]*

whatever happened to the sleepy Mexican
the smiley guy you met last summer
on the "Amigou Country" cruise, remember?
whatever happened to the great host
the helpful *kimozabe*
the sexy *mariachi* with pencil *mostachio*
the chubby cartoon character
you enjoyed so much in last Sunday's paper?
whatever happened to Speedy *González*

Border Brujo

Fritou Banditou, Johnny *McTaco, Pancho de Nacho,*
los treis caballerous, Ricardou Mont'lban
the *Baja Marimba* Band y sus *cantina* girls?
when did they disappear?
were they deported back to Mexicorama?
how? through Mexicannabis Airlines
& who let these troublemakers in?
are they for real? 'cause
I want to witness a real representation...

[His voice goes back to normal.]

hmmm, how ironic
I represent you
yet, you don't represent me

& you think you still have the power to define?
please...
please...
please...

XXII
[He speaks in a very elegant & soft-spoken manner.]

please don't touch me
I've got typhoid & *malaria*
don't dare touch me
I haven't been documented yet
I'm still an illegal alien
my back is wet
my nipples are hard
I'm ready to fight
I'm ready to rape
don't like me too much
'cause I'm a drug smuggling
welfare recipient-to-be
sexist communist car thief
fanatically devoted to the overthrow
of the U.S. government & the art world

[Pause]

no, just kiddin'
don't listen to me
I'm just a deterritorialized *"chilango"*
who claims to be a Chicano
& I'm not even eligible for amnesty
'cause I never documented my work
the only photos of my performances
are in the archives of the FBI
& I'm a bit too shy to ask them for copies
can anyone document me please?
can anyone take a photo of this memorable occasion?
come on, for the archives of border culture
for the history of performance art
can anyone be so kind as to authenticate my existence?

[He freezes for 20 seconds]

XXIII
*[Soundtrack: old instrumental blues.
He speaks like a "macuarro."]*

cameras 1 & 2 rolling
música maestro¡

[Music doesn't start]

¡ *músicaıı pss, que pasó?...pos nos la echamos sin música*

[Music finally begins.]

I was born in the middle of a movie set
they were shooting *"La Migra Contra El Príncipe Chichimeca"*
I was literally born in the middle of a battle
I'm almost an aborigine you know
a Hollywood Indian, *ajjuua!*
me dicen el Papantla Flyer
de la Broadway, bien tumbado

Border Brujo

'cause I love to show my balls to strangers
& to talk dirty to *gringas feministas*
& if it wasn't for the fact that I've read
too much Foucault & Baudrillard
& Fuentes & Subirats & Roger Bartra
& other writers you haven't even heard of
I could fulfill your expectations much better
if it wasn't for the fact that I wrote
this text on a MacIntosh
& I couldn't even memorize it all
& I shot my rehearsals with a Sony-8
I would really fulfull your expectations
le bon savage du Mexique
l'enfant terrible de la frontiere

> XXIV
> *[Soundtrack: Ry Cooder's "Canción Mixteca."*
> *He speaks with an unbearably snobbish accent.]*

oui, oui, oui
Mexique ooh la la
Chingada da-da
les enfants de la chingada
México rrromantic México
paraíso para tizos
para todos tifoidea
Chili Ortega pa' la güera
muchiou machou el muchiachou
ay, que rrico gaspachou
oh, pardon
don Giovani tampocou Mexicani?
from where?
São Paolo, Manila or Cuernavaca?

> *[He changes voice to that of a drunk tourist.]*

well, I don't care
it's all the same
the world is filled with colorful creatures

like me, like them
I simply adore Mexico
its fleshy *señoritas*
with humongous black eyes
walking down *Revolución*
like hundreds of thousands of *Carmen Mirandas*
with *sombrero grandi* & "Coppertone"
& man, they sure don't complain about *machismo*
they love it!!
porqui let's face it,
el machou Mexicanou no ser tan machou como el texanou

XXV

[Super-flamboyant Latino accent & exaggerated gestures]

please, check my pronounciation

I'm a child of the fallen Latin American oligarchy
I dream of a beautiful beautiful condo
in Coronado or Key West
away from my homeland in turmoil

I dream of a disinfected environment
one that only my memory can inhabit
& only the memories I want

she dreams of a beautiful suburb
somewhere in the periphery of her fears
she's tired of suffering
she lost her man in Santiago
her son in Guatemala
her daughter raped by a U.S. marine

she walked all the way from Tegucigalpa
she came to ask for an explanation
can anyone explain to her why?

*[A pre-recorded text in an Indian language
will continue throughout the next text.]*

Border Brujo

XXVI
[He switches to a "redneck" accent, speaks through megaphone.]

"no, no, too didactic"...
too romantic, too, too...

[He barks.]

not experimental enough
not inter-dizzy enough

[He barks again.]

looks like...

[He barks.]

old-fashioned Anglo stuff
I mean not enough...*picante*
not enough *bravadou & passionadou*
I want *mucho* more
I want to see García Márquez in 3-D
a post posty rendition of *Castaneda*
holographic shamans flying on stage
political massacres on multiple screens

[He gets progressively crazier.]

what's wrong with you pre-technological creatures?!
a-ffir-ma-ti-ve-ac-tion-pimps!
you can't even put together a good fuckin' video!!

[He breathes heavily & rests his head on the table]

XXVII
[He delivers text in broken English with an artificial smile.]

please check my pronunciation

this is the year of the Hispanic
Hispanics on MTV
Hispanics on Broadway
Hispanics in Hollywood
Hispanics in the Museum of Modern Art
Hispanics in. . . . .
Hispanics in the Calendar Section
Hispanics in Ripley's Believe It Or Not
Hispanics in Congress
Hispanics in General Dynamics
Hispanics in the Border Patrol
Hispanics in the Federal Jail
Hispanics in Skid Row
Hispanics in AIDS clinics
Hispanics in the cemetery
Hispanics in different sizes
buy one/get one for free
it's in, it's hot, it's cheap, it's durable
& like the bumpersticker says
"A TRUE HISPANIC IS NOT JUST YOUR PANIC
BUT EVERYONE'S PANIC"

[Pause]

as I was saying
thanks to marketing
& not to civil rights
we are the new generation

[Pause.]

of laboratory rats & experimental patients.

[He begins to cut coke/speak like a druggie]

. . .at night
alone in my condo
when I pray to my 3-D virgin
it's strange you know

Border Brujo

I'm happy yet I feel like killing myself
so I take more pills to fall asleep
the pills you sent me last month are terrific
they make me forget all the pain
& alienation I thought I used to feel
they make me feel part of it all
with them I feel one with California
one with the art world
& a thousand within myself
justo a tu imágen y semejanza
so I turn on the radio...

XXVIII
[He grabs megaphone/speaks like a barker.]

alien-ation
alien action
alienated
álguien ate it
alien hatred
aliens out there
hay álguien out there!
"Aliens" the movie
"Aliens" the album
"Cowboys vs. Aliens"
"Bikers vs. Aliens"
"The Wet Back from Mars"
"The Mexican Transformer & his Radio-active *Torta*"
"The Conquest of *Tenochtitlan*" by Spielberg
"The Reconquest of *Aztlán*" by Monty Python
"The Brown Wave vs. the Micro Wave"
"Invaders from the South vs. the San Diego *Padres*
reinforced by the San Diego Police
reinforced by your ignorance dear San Diegan..."

good morning
this is Radio Latino FM
spoiling your breakfast as always

[The remainder of this text is pre-recorded. He sub-vocalizes.]

*efectivamente, anoche asesinaron
a un niño mexicano de escasos 8 años
la patrulla fronteriza asegura
que se trata de "peligroso asaltante"
a continuación, más noticias en inglés:*

the Mexican fly is heading North
the Mexican fly is coming to destroy your crops
the Mexican fly is now in Chihuahua
there's no insecticide for the Mexican fly
no antidote for your fear of otherness
the Simpson-Rodino bill is an emergency plan to regulate
    your fears
some call it an act of political fumigation
the Amnesty Program has been designed to legalize otherness
for otherness keeps leaking into the country into your psyche

dear listener/dear audience
your country is no longer yours
your relationship with otherness has reached a point of crisis
you love me/you hate me
you are in good company
but you don't know it yet
the Mexican fly will be coming soon to a garden near you

good evening
this is Radio Latino FM
interrupting your coitus as always

*[He sings an Indian song & covers his face with
the hair of the wig.]*

XXIX
[Soundtrack: New Age percussion. He enters into a trance.]

I see Tenochtitlan Island
resting peacefully on the surface of a daiquiri

Border Brujo

I see the Aztec warrior in a strait jacket
facing a 100 year sentence in Chino
I see the Spanish landowner & the American tourist
getting wasted at *Margarita*'s Village
I see the border guards masturbating & vomiting
under the border fog
under the very fog that covers us right now
I see the first sparks of the 2nd Mexican Independence
& the final kicks of a drowning saurus
I see other more personal things
like friendly women & friendly men
really trying to understand
but despite of all these visions
estoy triste en país ajeno
estoy muy triste en país ajeno
estamos tristes en país ajeno
país de todos/país de nadie
& there's nothing you can do to ease my pain
nothing sadder than a Mexican artist in Southern California
under the present Administration
nothing is really administered but death

[He speaks in tongues.]

I mean, death as a "lifestyle"
death as a media celebrity
death as a mandatory practice
la gran calaca güera que todo lo gobierna

[He speaks in tongues.]

in order to operate without physical repercussions
I chose the temporary safety of the art world

[He continues to speak in tongues.]

XXX
*[He screams over the heads of the audience,
as if wanting to reach someone far away.]*

hermano de allá
de hasta allá abajo
si tan sólo supieras lo que es
pasarse una noche solitario
en un motel de Alabama
en una cantina de Oxnard *o* Detroit
caminar por las calles desiertas y peligrosas
de Marin County *o* Pasadena
amar en Nueva York
con el temor de un contagio mortal
y por si fuera poco
sentir la lúz del helicóptero en Imperial Beach
la voz forastera por la espalda...

[He freezes for 20 seconds.]

XXXI
[He speaks in very broken English.]

no, I have no green card
I was illegally hired by this gallery
the director might receive employer's sanctions
the INS might raid my audience
one of these nights
one of them might even shoot me
from the audience
perhaps tonight
one never knows nowadays
anything can happen in America
we are so fuckin' vulnerable in America
I'm scared therefore you exist
so look out for me
I'm going through the Big Smoke
I'm going through the Big Smoke
& so are you

[He walks around the audience speaking in tongues.
He suddenly stops, and seems very irritated.]

Border Brujo

there is a Border Patrol agent in the audience
can he please identify himself?
can you please identify yourself?

            [Long pause.]

!cobarde!!

            XXXII
     [He uses the megaphone.]

dear friends
let me ask you a few questions
has anyone ever crossed a border illegally?
has anyone ever smuggled any "illegal substances" or radical literature?
have you ever harbored or hired an "illegal alien"
have you ever worked illegally yourself?
have you ever visited a "communist country" or a transvestite cantina?
have you ever joined an anti-American organization named......?
have you ever engaged in sexually illicit practices?
come on, be honest
this is just a performance
no big deal
I've been asked myself each of these questions
at least a couple hundred times
& I've been violently frisked at least 20 times
for not having answered them

   [He puts down the megaphone, raises his hands & freezes.]

& you ask me
"are you implying that the US is a police state?"
but I can only answer in *náhuatl*

      [He answers in an Indian dialect.]

but you insist
"isn't California the ultimate utopia for Latinos?"
& this time I answer with a violent question
"isn't Disneyland the capital of California?"
& you interrupt me with a knife
"...but Guillermo, you're cheating
you're exercising your political freedom"
& I think for a second, "hmmm"
& reply "sure..."
but how many people are here tonight
to listen to my political freedom?
& we begin to count them
& as we count them in Spanish
we begin to wonder about freedom in America
& the show goes on
& the critic over there is falling asleep
wondering why Latinos are so bloody dramatic

XXXIII
[He lights a joint and speaks as though he were "high."]

our moment arrived
we did have a chance to speak out
but we hesitated
& someone up there
unplugged the lights...& the camera
before we even realized it

[He smokes more pot. His voice becomes muddy.]

the "quebequization" of the Southwest
was effectively coopted by the NSA
& our communities were fragmented
by the asymmetrical distribution of funding & space
we all know it...& suffer it

*[He snorts fictional drugs. Speaks like a junkie,
moving his head like a pendulum.]*

Border Brujo

today, once again
we are alone
like in the early days
alone like children in the forest
like Chicano performance artists
in Anglo alternative spaces
we are alone & waiting
like the popular *corrido* says
"some are waiting for Amnesty
& others for the guillotine blade"

*[He repeats this phrase several times as if totally drugged out.
Then he puts on a wrestler's mask & stands up.]*

XXXIV
[He speaks like a hard core political activist.]

"whatever happened to the leaders?" you ask me
some died of a heart attack
with a little help from the CIA
some are mortally wounded by the media
& others paralyzed by chemical nostalgia
a few created an impenetrable bureaucracy
emulating their enemies
or found refuge & comfort in the university spa

today (date)
standing on the edge
of the 20th century cliff
I finally dare to ask you
where are all my Chicano *compadres?*
I can't accept that they all went crazy like me
or yuppie like some of you
can't accept the Indian leaders are still in jail
can't believe the Puerto Rican *independentistas* are still in jail
after all these years
still in jail in America
& you worry about Nelson Mandela?

[Long pause.]

& you worry about Lech Walesa?

[Long pause.]

& you worry about cigarette smoking?

[He cries for a few seconds & covers his face.]

XXXV
[He continues like a hard core political activist.]

last night at the "Main Intersection"
someone told me
that all we want is
access to the suburbs
access to the museums
to the City Council
to the media
to your girlfriend
that all-we-want-is-access
access!, access!, access!!
well, I'm sorry to disappoint you "someone"
all we want is to go back
but for the moment
there's nowhere to go back to

[Pause. He changes to normal voice.]

our past was destroyed by your government
therefore dear "someone"
this is our land for the moment
& you gotta share the pie
to regain your peace of mind

[He speaks in tongues, then switches to normal voice.]

& you insist on asking me

what am I doing here?
como podré explicártelo
sin ofenderte...
if Spalding Gray can go to Cambodia
why can't I come to.......?

XXXVI
[Soundtrack: Rossini or Beethoven. He speaks through megaphone.]

tonight, I am the one who determines
the exact nature of our relation
even if only for one night
I SAY:
you are no longer my spectator
you are my object of adoration
your country is losing weight & size
your skin is losing its privilege
your crisis is graver than mine
I SAY:
ciudadano del mentado primer mundo
you have a friend in me
a solid but critical friend
a friend who will never betray you
but never again will accept
your asymmetrical conditions
I SAY:
generic citizenship
Norteamérica has grown
back to its original size
from *Yucatán* to Greenland
from Michigan to *Michoacán*
I toast to *Nuestra América*
from the *Papago* to the punk
I toast to the beginning of an era
a true multi-cultural society
from ritual art to "neo-geo"
I toast in equal terms with you
my dear *Anglosaxican* partner

waspano de 2nda o 3a generación
in my performance country
República de Arteamérica
you're just a minority
but you have some rights
like the right to listen respectfully
& as long as you continue
to fear *moi* or desire me
without proportion to my dignity
then, my dear involuntary neighbor
entropy will keep creeping
like magma into your tract home
into your troubled spirit
& I won't be there to rescue you
from the flood of your guilt

[He puts down the megaphone.]

& you, my dear *negro, latino, indígena, oriental*
or hybrid in between
you're next
like it or not
you have till January 1st of 92
to incorporate this country into the world
to turn the continent upside down
& infect English with Spanish & Japanese
and many other *verboten imbricalingüis*
remember
you have 3 years to get your shit together

XXXVII
[Soundtrack: "Ojos Españoles" by Los Xochimilcas.
He speaks like a smooth-talker, while applying orange or red
makeup.]

so, my dear audience
we are finally in the same room
even if only for an evening
we are truly conversing right now

Border Brujo

in your language, but conversing after all...
so I mean to ask you
where is the threshhold of your desire?
Baghdad, Sao Paulo, Berlin, Tangier,
Calcutta, Tijuana, Ibiza, La Chingada
where are your memories running loose?
in which bed
in whose arms
on which stage
in which language are you dreaming?
in Spanish, Jamaican English or Persian?
where will your permanent home be erected?
in Jakarta, Managua or Oro Preto
perhaps somewhere on the shores of Cataluña
beyond the borders of panic & boredom?
I envy your capability to desire
I really do

[His voice changes to that of a drunk.]

I'm here in prison
right in the center of the wound
right in the crack of the 2 countries
I am a prisoner of thought
a prisoner of art
a prisoner of a media war
I'm each & every bad guy in the film
a one-man film so to speak
they call me El Corny, El Slickoid
El Nahuál Conceptual, El Suddenly *Violento*
El Channy Fumigamitos
I'm getting tired *corazón*
where *demonios* are you?
I want to read you something from my hear
are you coming to visit me tonight?
are they going to let you in?

XXXVIII
[Music continues. He speaks like a stylized Pachuco.]

hey!
my Spider Babe
my Surfin' *Loca*
my Mambo Jane
my Bless Me *Ultima*
la Jazzercise
házmela buena
la Nena Radioactiva
la Biker *Lacandona*
la Corporate *Chingona*
la "búscame a horcajadas en noches de neón"
la gimme those *besitos* across the border fence
ay, ay, Pantera Feminista
la gran Bruja Marxista
abráxame retuérxeme
soy tu loco encaramado al muslo izquierdo
y no me suelto por nada
soy el pendejo permanente
que llevas tatuado en una chichi
la izquierda, la grandota
y no me borro
ay, Batichica de Mexicali
let me know if you are coming back soon
for I'm tired of fighting *la migra* by myself
ay, my little brown self
is almost non-existant tonight
ay, la pinche velita se me apaga

XXXIX
[He drinks from the shampoo bottle. Speaks like a drunk, covering his face with his hands.]

I hate to say it but we failed

[Pause.]

we are still alive but...we failed
still awake, sort of
but kind'a clumsy & fuzzy

Border Brujo

the food tastes like shit
the music is awful
it's all been done before
one artist replaces the other
one minority replaces the other
& the other, other, other, others
next year Latinos are "out"
& albino Rumanians are "in"
therefore my dear audience
I'm going back to Hell
en camión de tres estrellas
como vine
back to the origins maextro

XL

[He begins to walk into the audience, while delivering final text as a merolico. He holds two baskets; one is empty & the other is filled with food & ritual objects.]

but before I go back
ladies & gentlemen
I'm going to ask you to give me
whatever you no longer need
please feel free to get rid of everything
you wish you didn't have:
money, IDs, ideas, your keys, your sins
your telephone number, your credit card
your leather jacket, your contact lenses, etc.
please make sure that whatever you give me
you're prepared to never see again.
Some objects I will bury right on the US-México border ditch.
& others will become part of my travelling altar
damas y caballeros... aflojen!!

FIN.

BIOGRAPHICAL NOTES

MARJORIE AGOSIN was born in Chile in 1955 and came to the U.S. in 1971. She is currently a professor in the Spanish Department of Wellesley College. Her poetry is refreshing and laced with humor, even when engaged in serious themes. Her topics range from the erotic to the dark playfulness of life to torture and rebellion.

In her six published books of poetry, Agosín has developed an unflinching, direct voice. She has published three books of criticism: on Pablo Neruda, on Maria Luisa Bombal and on the metaphors of women writers. Among her books of poetry are: *Chile, Gemidos y Cantares* (1977), *Conchali* (1980), *Silencio que se deja or* (1984) and *Brujas y algo mas* (1985).

CLARIBEL ALEGRIA was born in Nicaragua in 1924 but was raised in El Salvador. She earned her Bachelor's degree in Philosophy and Letters from George Washington University in the 1940s. Alegria has lived in Mexico, Chile, Uruguay, Mallorca and, since the victory of the Sandinista Front for National Liberation in 1979, in Nicaragua. Her commitment to social change has kept her in exile from El Salvador.

Being America

Alegría's writing has a strong testimonial quality; she has referred to her work as "letras de emergencia" (emergency or crisis writing). She is actively concerned with the status of women in Central America, and with the need to address the entrenched prejudices of the social structure. Her novels include *Cenizas de Izalco* (1966), *Album familiar* (1982), and *Luisa in Realityland* (1987). Among her ten books of poetry is *Sobrevivo* (1978), winner of the prestigious Casa de las Americas prize. With her husband Darwin J. Flakoll she has co-authored testimonial works about women, political prisoners and the history of Nicaragua.

CARLOS CAPELAN was born in Uruguay in 1948 but left that country in exile during the military dictatorship and currently lives in Sweden. His work is surreal and psychoanalytical, somewhat in the tradition of Jose Luis Cuevas, the Mexican expressionist. He is an excellent drawing artist, and received one of the few prizes of the second Bienal of Havana. Capelan is interested in rituals and death, and has done extensive studies on those themes. He has exhibited throughout Europe and Latin America.

WILFREDO CHIESA is a Puerto Rican abstract painter who has lived in Boston for nine years. He has exhibited his work extensively in Colombia, Puerto Rico, the U.S., Panama, the Dominican Republic, Paris and Cuba, and has taught in Puerto Rico, Colombia and Boston. Chiesa has become a leading figure in the Boston Latino cultural community.

RITA EDER was born in Mexico in 1943. She holds an M.A. from the National Autonomous University of Mexico (UNAM), as well as an M.A. in Art History from Ohio State University. Her primary interest is in Latin American art, particularly that of Mexico. Eder has published widely in magazines, newspapers and scholarly journals in Mexico, Brazil, the U.S., Spain, Germany, Colombia and Peru. She curated the Mexican entry to the Bienal of Paris in 1980, and produces a weekly TV program on art criticism for Mexico's Channel 11.

MARTIN ESPADA, a Puerto Rican poet originally from Brooklyn, is the author of two poetry collections: *The Immigrant Iceboy's*

Biographical Notes

Bolero and *Trumpets from the Islands of their Eviction*. His work has also appeared in many journals and anthologies, including *River Styx, The Greenfield Review, Hispanics in the United States, Vol. II* and *Editor's Choice, Vol. II*. He is also the editor of "Ten Poets: A Latino Supplement," in *Hanging Loose* magazine.

Espada has been awarded a Massachusetts Artists Fellowship (1984), a National Endowment for the Arts Fellowship (1986), a Boston Contemporary Writer's Award (1987) and the Rosalie Boyle Award (1987). Espada currently lives in Boston, where he works as a tenant lawyer through the Su Clínica program of Suffolk University Law School, and teaches a course on Latino poetry at Wheelock College.

GUILLERMO GOMEZ-PENA is an interdisciplinary artist/writer, born and raised in Mexico City. He studied Spanish Literature at the Universidad Iberoamericana and Linguistics at the National Autonomous University of Mexico (UNAM). Later he obtained B.F.A. and M.F.A. degrees in Art/Post Studio Art at the California Institute for the Arts.

In 1981 Gómez-Peña formed Poyesis Genetica Troupe, a multimedia performance project focusing on the cultural/political relationships between Latin America and the U.S. In 1984 he co-founded the Border Art Workshop (BAW/TAF), a leading group who utilize the San Diego-Tijuana border as an artistic/intellectual laboratory to produce bicultural art and social dialogue through multiple media such as film, video, performance, installations, books, radio, etc. In 1987 he co-founded and edited the bilingual interdisciplinary magazine *La Linea Quebrada (The Broken Line)*.

ALFREDO JAAR was born in Chile in 1956 and arrived in New York in 1982, where he currently lives. A Guggenheim recipient, he works on installations based on political and social subject matter related to Latin America. Jaar's work, sometimes simplistically called "conceptual," has been shown in numerous solo and group exhibitions, including the 1986 Venice Biennale and the 1989 Magiciens de la Terre exhibition in Paris.

According to Jaar, public art is not public because it is in the streets but because it is generated by public events. "Artists should not create public works to last," he says, "We should not impose our esthetics, or even our ethics, on people."

NORBERTO JAMES was born in the Dominican Republic, and moved to Boston in 1983. He received a *licenciatura* in Hispanic Languages and Literature from the University of Havana (1978) and an M.A. degree from Boston University (1985), where he is now completing his doctoral work. Among his work are four published books of poetry: *Sobre la marcha* (1969), *La provincia sublevada* (1972), *Vivir* (1982) and *Hago constar* (1983).

MARTA LAMAS was born in Mexico in 1947. An anthropologist and journalist, she was one of the founders of *Fem* magazine (1976), and has long been active in Mexico's feminist movement. She has taught Political Science ("Women and Politics") at the National Autonomous University of Mexico (UNAM) as well as "The Anthropology of Women" at La Escuela Nacional de la Antropologia e Historia (National School of Anthropology and History).

Lamas was a founder of "Mujeres en Accion Sindical" (MAS), a coalition of women workers, in 1985 after the earthquake, and was instrumental in setting up the Centro de Apoyo a la Mujer Obrera (Center for the Support of Working Women) in 1986 and its newspaper *Nosotras*. She has been a regular contributor to the political magazine *Nexxus* since 1986.

FRANCISCO MENDEZ-DIEZ is a Cuban-born painter and printmaker who has been working in Boston for the past 14 years. Méndez-Díez has committed himself for over a decade to bringing the work of Latino artists to greater prominence in the U.S. His images frequently confront the painful history that belongs to Latin America, acting both as witness and as commentator.

Méndez-Díez has won several awards, has been artist-in-residence at numerous institutions and has exhibited at the Boston Museum of Fine Arts, the Bienal of Printmaking in Puerto Rico and many galleries.

GERARDO MOSQUERA is an art critic, curator and writer born and living in Cuba. As a spokesperson and major theoretician for the Cuban artistic avant garde, he has sought to give system and

Biographical Notes

theoretical consistency to a new generation of young artists that is currently working in Cuba.

Currently Mosquera is advisor to the Centro Wifredo Lam in Havana, and co-organizer of the Bienal in the same city. He has also studied and written on the subject of Afro-Cuban art and rituals. His books include *Exploraciones en la plastica cubana* and a more recent volume of short stories.

LUIS FELIPE NOE was born in Buenos Aires, Argentina in 1933. He was a member of the "Otra Figuracion" (Another Figuration) group, a tendency which had built (and took off) from the neo-Expressionists. Noe recently returned to Argentina, after a long period of exile in Paris.

Noe has written several books about art and Latin America, including the 1965 *Anti-Estetica,* and has received two Guggenheim fellowships. During the early 1960s he challenged accepted painting rules and notions of beauty and did environmental paintings preceding Larry Rivers' "History of the Russian Revolution" and the work of Red Grooms. After not painting for nine years, Noe has resumed his work in drawing and painting, using mixed media and a large format to depict historical and mythological themes.

JULIO ORTEGA, born in 1942, is Peru's leading literary intellectual. His criticism is known to readers in the U.S. through such magazines as *TriQuarterly, Yale Literary Review,* and *Texas Quarterly.* His critical work, which has dealt with poets such as Cesar Vallejo, Cesar Moro, Lezama Lima and Neruda, and novelists García Márquez, Carpentier and Cortázar, has also been published in Spanish in such prestigious journals as *Revista Iberoamericana, Plural, Eco* and *Quimera.*

Long-recognized as an authority in the field of utopian literature as a result of his novel *Tierra en el dia,* Ortega has created a utopian text with roots in tradition yet radically modified by his contemporary vision. Awarded the Guggenheim Fellowship in 1974, Ortega has taught at Yale, the University of Texas/Austin, Brandeis and, currently, Brown University.

CRISTINA PACHECO was born in Guanajuato, Mexico in 1941. Her family moved to Mexico City when she was seven. She studied Letters at the National Autonomous University of Mexico (UNAM) and began her journalistic career with the newspaper *El Popular* (later renamed *El Dia*) in 1960. Pacheco also worked for two women's magazines, *La Familia* and *La Mujer de hoy*. A tireless journalist, she has contributed to the following papers: *El Universal, El Sol de Mexico, Uno Mas Uno, La Jornada* and, for the last 11 years, the weekly *Siempre*. She has published five books of stories, among them *Para vivir aqui* (1983), *Zona de desastre* (1985) about the September 1985 earthquake and *La ultima noche de tigre* (1987). A book of 30 interviews with distinguished public figures, *Los duenos de la noche,* is due for publication.

ELENA PONIATOWSKA was born in Paris of Polish-Mexican background in 1933. At the age of eight, she immigrated with her parents to Mexico, where she has lived ever since. In the mid-1950s she began writing for newspapers, working on her own prose and poetry as well.

Poniatowska has written children's books (*Lilus Kikus*), short stories (*De Noche Vienes*) and testimonial novels. Her authentic and clear voice is one that is identified with the voice of the Mexican people. She is extremely adept at expressing the experiences of women, and by bringing history to life in individual portraits she forces her readers to reconsider the personal dimensions of otherwise distant events or situations. Her best-known works are: *Hasta No Verte, Jesus Mio* (Here's Looking At You, Jesus), 1969; *La Noche de Tlateloco* (Massacre in Mexico), 1973; *Querido Diego, te Abraza Quiela* (Dear Diego), 1978; and, *Gaby Brimmer,* 1979.

JUAN SANCHEZ is a Puerto Rican artist born in New York who uses his concern about the independence of Puerto Rico as a main subject. Combining painting, photography, newspaper clippings, glyphs from Taíno culture, religious imagery, flag motifs and written texts, Sánchez weaves a multi-layered fabric of meaning. Sánchez received a fellowship from the National Endowment for the Arts in 1983 and has exhibited widely in the U.S., Puerto Rico and Cuba.

LUIS RAFAEL SANCHEZ was born in Puerto Rico in 1936. He is

Biographical Notes

a novelist, playwright, short story writer, essayist, journalist and critic. His play *La pasion segun Antigona Pérez* was his first successful work, and *Cuerpa de camisa* is one of the best collections of short stories by a Puerto Rican author. His most popular novel, *La guaracha del Macho Camacho* (1976) was translated into English as *Macho Camacho's Beat* by Gregory Rabassa.

Sánchez's fiction is humorous, satirical and mordant, often poking fun at the social mores and political milieu of Puerto Rico. He currently teaches at the University of Puerto Rico.

CECILIA VICUNA, poet and artist, was born in Chile in 1948 and currently lives in New York. She has published six books of poetry, contributed to numerous anthologies and created major film and video works. She has also exhibited widely throughout Europe and the Americas.

In her art and poetry, Vicuña acknowledges the strong indigenous and mestizo presence in Chile, integrating it into European structures. Since her earliest works performed in nature in 1966, and since her earliest poems published in 1967, Vicuña has embraced what she calls "my Andean being, *mi andinidad*."

ALAN WEST was born in Havana, Cuba in 1953 and raised in Puerto Rico. He has a B.A. in Economics from Columbia University, and an M.A. in Latin American Literature from NYU. He has been a regular contributor to the magazines *Joven Cuba* and *Areíto,* and has published poetry, film and literary criticism in the U.S., Puerto Rico, Cuba, Nicaragua and Mexico. West has translated extensively, including work on film documentaries. A short collection of poetry, *En cinco tiempos* (1987), is his first book.

* * *

CRISTINA CARDALDA was born in Cuba in 1960 and was raised in Puerto Rico from the age of five. She has a Bachelor's degree in Envoronmental Design from the University of Puerto Rico and a Master's in Architecture from the Harvard Graduate School of Design. She won the NEA Award for Academic Excellence in 1984, and has published translations in the *Harvard Educational Review*.

Being America

COLA FRANZEN concentrates on translating work, mostly poetry, of four contemporary Latin American poets: Marjorie Agosín, Alicia Borinsky, Juan Cameron and Saul Yurkievich. Her translations include the following books: *Witches and Other Things (Brujas y algo mas), Scraps of Life: The Chilean Arpilleras and Zones of Pain (Las zonas del dolor),* all by Agosín. Forthcoming books include: *Poems of Arab Andalusia, Diary of A Voyage* (prison diary of the Chilean painter Guillermo Nunez) and *VERSE/transVERSE* (poems by Saul Yurkievich). Franzen lives in Cambridge, Massachusetts, and is an associate editor of *O.ARS.*

SOLEDAD GELLES is an interpreter and translator born in Peru and currently living in the Boston area. She holds a B.A. degree in translation from the Universidad Ricardo Palma in Lima, Peru and an M.A. in German Literature from Tufts University in Medford, Massachusetts. She has conducted anthropological fieldwork focusing on textiles in an Andean peasant community.

RACHEL WEISS is an artist, writer and organizer currently based in Boston. She has a B.A. from Marlboro College in Vermont and an M.F.A. from the Massachusetts College of Art, where she also worked for five years as the Coordinator of the Visiting Artists Program, of which this festival was part.

Weiss' work focuses on the development of a trans-cultural perspective and practice which depends for its success on close, collaborative relationships in projects involving artists, musicians, writers, activists and others from many cultures and locations. She is a consultant to numerous museums, and to artist-run and grass roots organizations. Her art work has been exhibited and/or performed throughout Europe and the U.S. and her writings on culture have appeared in various journals.

END NOTES

"Memory and Identity: Some Historical-Cultural Notes"
Elena Poniatowska

[1] Indigenous Mexican group

[2] José Enrique Rodó: Uruguayan essayist and writer (1871-1917), author of *Ariel, Los motivos de Proteo* and other works; an outstanding representative of Latin American modernism.

[3] Domingo Faustino Sarmiento: Argentinian politician and writer (1811-1888). Was President (1868), and founded the Astronomy Observatory of Córdoba. He wrote *Facundo: Civilización o barbarie,* a book which took a highly laudatory view of U.S. and European civilization.

[4] Manuel Bilbao: Chilean writer (1827-1895), author of many novels including *El inquisidor mayor* and *El pirata de Guayas.*

[5] José Martí: Cuban writer, politician and leader of the independence struggle against Spain (1835-1895). A brilliant poet, essayist and journalist, and a seminal figure in Cuban history who was an important influence on Fidel Castro and the Cuban Revolution.

[6]Andrés Bello: Born in Venezuela (1781) and died in Chile (1865). Bello was a writer, philologist, poet, politician and legal scholar. He wrote Chile's Civil Code (1855), and was a close ally of Simón Bolívar.

[7]Juan Montalvo: Ecuadorian writer (1832-1889) and political figure. He published numerous essays and speeches.

[8]José Carlos Mariátegui: Peruvian essayist, sociologist and political figure (1895-1930). He founded Perú's Communist Party in the 1920s, and his *Seven Essays for Understanding Peruvian Reality* is still considered a valuable work.

[9]José de Vasconcelos: Mexican writer and politician (1881-1959). Was Minister of Education in the 1920s and wrote many books on philosophy, history and esthetics, as well as short stories and memoirs.

[10]José María Morelos: Mexican priest and patriot (1765-1815). A leader in the struggle for Mexican independence from Spain, Morelos was captured, and shot by a Spanish firing squad.

[11]Argentinian-Paraguayan War (The War of the Triple Alliance): 1864-1870. The war cost Paraguay half of its population and caused a total economic collapse of the country.

[12]*Hasta no verte Jesús mío*: novel by Elena Poniatowska. Published in México by Ediciones Era, 1969. It is now in its 26th edition.

[13]Language spoken by the Aztecs in México.

[14]Language and culture of the indigenous population of Perú, parts of Ecuador and Bolivia, descended from the Incas.

[15]Literally, "The kid from house #8." A TV show about a poor boy from the barrios, and the situations he gets into. He's a little on the dumb side— and it's there that the comic side of his character derives.

[16]A popular TV figure throughout Latin America, well-liked by children in particular. Although played by an actor well into his 40s (or more), he is something of a cross betwen Pee Wee Herman and Roger Rabbit. He dresses in a cape, and has head gear similar to an insect.

[17]Indigenous population of Chile. Their collective resistance to colonization was documented in the epic poem "La Araucaria" about the Spanish conquest of Chile (written by Alonso de Ercilla, 1533-1594). The poem is an unusual document in that it offers a sensitive portrayal of the suffering of the indigenous peoples.

[18]Charismatic, authoritarian strongmen

[19]Or, "Río Grande" to North Americans.

"Art and Identity in Latin America"
Rita Eder

[1]In 1970, under the auspices of UNESCO, experts from different Latin American countries came together under the guidelines of the UNESCO program "to consider America as a whole, integrated by the actual national political formations," to discuss the following problems. They were: 1) The Situation of Latin America in the World Today; 2) Roots, Assimilation and Conflicts; 3) Art and Society. This meeting resulted in the publication of *América Latina en sus artes,* Siglo XXI, 1974. Following this model other meetings took place with the goal of bringing together a Latin American thought or perspective on art. This effort yielded another important result, the First Latin American Biennale in São Paolo (1978), with an overarching theme of "Myth and Magic." There were no startling conclusions from these efforts, but new fields of research and study opened up, the most important being the unshakeable necessity to bring popular arts into the fine arts system. In this sense, studies by Nestor García Canclini are well known: *Popular Art and Society in Latin America (Arte popular y sociedad en América Latina),* México, Grijalbo, 1977; *Popular Cultures in Capitalism (Las culturas populares en el capitalismo),* México, Nueva Imagen, 1982; and, Mirko Lauer's *A Critique of Arts and Crafts (Crítica de la artesanía),* Lima, Centro de Estudios y Promoción del Desarrollo, DESCO, 1982; "Crafts and Capitalism in Peru" ("Artesanía y capitalismo en el Perú"), *Foreign Trade (Comercio exterior),* México, Vol. XXVIII, #8, 1977. Another important contribution is Juan Acha's extensive work *Art and Society in Latin America (América Latina en su arte),* México, Fondo de Cultura Económica (three volumes, 1979, 1981, 1983). While Acha has a lot to say on how the social impinges on the symbolic, he underlines the need of aesthetics in an analysis intrinsic to the study of art. This two track look at artistic production has resulted in a socio-aesthetics, to use Acha's phrase.

²On this point see the following: Antenor Orrego, "¿Cuál es la cultura que creará América Latina?" ("What is the Culture which Latin America will Create?"), *Amanta,* Lima, Perú, #14, 1928, pp. 3-4; Victor Raúl Haya de la Torre, "Romain y Rolland y la América Latina" ("Romain and Rolland and Latin America"), op. cit., #2, 1926, pp. 12-13; José Carlos Mariátegui, "Arte, decadencia y revolución" ("Art, Decadence and Revolution"), ibid., #3, 1926, pp. 3-4; José Vasconcelos, "El nacionalismo en América Latina" ("Nationalism in Latin America"), ibid., #4, 1926, pp. 13-16, and ibid., #5, 1927, pp. 22-24.

³In his article "Nationalism and Latin America," op. cit., Vasconcelos states that the strongest unifying element in Latin America is that of language, and this includes Portuguese: "Portuguese and Spanish, two Iberoromantic languages, easily interchangeable and among us a substitute for that Babel of different languages which characterize Europe."

⁴Sheldon Williams, *Voodoo and the Art of Haiti,* U.K., Morland Lee Ltd., 1969. According to the established version, it was the North American De Witt Peters who acted as the catalyst for the movement in Haitian painting, by opening the Centre d'Art in Port-au-Prince in 1945. In his book, Williams makes reference to Hyppolite but also refers to 40 other painters of exceptional quality who appeared between 1945 and 1969.

⁵Andre Breton, *Le Surrealisme et la Peinture (Surrealism and Painting),* Paris, Gallimard, 1965. Héctor Hyppolite is mentioned on pages 308-312, and Wifredo Lam on pages 169-172.

⁶See Edmundo Desnoes, "Wifredo Lam: Black and Blue" ("Wifredo Lam: azul y negro") in *Plural,* México, #90, March 1979, pp. 3941 and Fernando Ortíz, "Wifredo Lam y su obra a través de significados críticos" ("Wifredo Lam and His Work through the Eyes of Criticism") in Antonio Nuñez Jiménez' *Wifredo Lam,* Havana, Letras Cubanas, 1982, pp. 11-37. See also Adelaida de Juan, "Las artes plásticas en las Antillas, México y América Central" ("The Visual Arts in the Antilles, Mexico and Central America") in Manuel Moreno Fraginals (editor), *Africa en América Latina (Africa in Latin America),* México, Siglo XXI, 1977, pp. 304-324.

⁷Alejo Carpentier, "Problemática de la actual novela latinoamericana" ("Problems in the Current Latin American Novel") in *Literatura y conciencia política en América Latina (Literature and Political Conscience in Latin America),* Madrid, Alberto Corazón, 1969, p. 20.

⁸Gonzalo Celorio, *El surrealismo y lo real maravailloso americano (Sur-*

End Notes

realism and Latin American Magic Realism), México, Sep-Setentas, 1976, p. 67.

[9]Alejo Carpentier, "El reino de este mundo" ("The Kingdom of This World") in *Dos Novelas (Two Novels)*, Havana, Letras Cubanas, 1979.

[10]Juan Acha, "el geometrismo reciente y latinoamericano" ("Recent Latin American Geometrism"), in Jorge Alberto Manrique, et. al., *El geometrismo mexicano (Mexican Geometrism)*, México, Instituto de Investigaciones Estéticas, UNAM, 1977, pp. 31-49.

[11]Ferreira Gullar, "Vanguardia e sudesenvolvimiento" ("Vanguard and Underdevelopment"), Rio de Janeiro, Civilizacao Brasileira, 1978.

[12]Marta Traba, *Dos decádas vulnerables en el arte de América Latina (Two Vulnerable Decades of Latin American Art)*, México, Siglo XXI, 1973.

[13]Rita Eder, "El arte público en México: Los Grupos": ("Public Art in Mexico: The Groups") in *Artes Visuales,* México, Museo de Arte Moderno, #23; and "Razón y sinrazón del arte efímero: algunos ejemplos latinoamericanos" ("Reason and Unreason in Ephemeral Art: Some Latin American Examples"), *Plural,* México, #90, March 1979, pp. 27-34.

[14]René Depestre, "Saludo y despido a la negritud" ("Hello and Goodbye to Negritude") in Manuel Moreno Fraginals (ed.), *Africa en América Latina,* México, Siglo XXI, p. 341.

[15]Federico Morais, *Artes plásticas na América Latina do transe a transitório (The Visual Arts in Latin America: From Anguish to the Transitory)*, Río de Janeiro, Civilizacao Brasileira, pp. 13-14.

"Our Little Region"
Claribel Alegria

[1]FMLN, or Frente Farabundo Martí para la Liberacion Nacional, is the main guerrila organization fighting for the liberation of El Salvador.

[2]The right wing ARENA party was declared the victor of the March 1989 elections; less than 50% of the electorate voted, and the election was widely criticized by observers and marred by incidents of violence. [Ed.]

[3] Somoza's bunker, where he hid in the final months of his regime.

[4] Anti-Sandinista forces led by Eden Pastora.

[5] Coalition led by Guillermo Ungo and Rubén Zamora

[6] Publication is scheduled for September 1989 by Curbstone Press.

"Plastic Arts in Cuba"
Gerardo Mosquera

[1] This text was not delivered at the conference session, since Mosquera's arrival in the U.S. was delayed.

[2] Roger Bastide was a French sociologist/anthropologist who dedicated himself to the study of the African religious presence in Latin America, particularly *candomblé,* the Brazilian equivalent of *santería.* His best-known works are *Les religions africaines au Brésil* (Presses Universitaires de France/PUF, 1960) and *Les Amériques noires* (Payot, Paris, 1967)

[3] A palero's cauldron.

[4] One of the names given to the spirit living inside the palero's cauldron. A palero is a priest of Palo, a sect based on the beliefs and magical practices of the Kongo, from the part of Africa now known as Zaire.

[5] Hart, the Cuban Minister of Culture, was a member of the early and central revolutionary cadre. Hart was married to the legendary patriot Haydée Santamaría.

[6] Landmark exhibition in Havana presenting the work of the young Cuban artists for the first time.

[7] "Rectification" is the term used to describe the return to more traditional socialist economic policies called for in 1986 by Fidel Castro.

"Transcript of Remarks by Cecilia Vicuña"

[1] These remarks followed a performance/reading by Vicuña.

End Notes

"Marjorie Agosin"

[1] Translated by Cola Franzen

[2] Translated by Naomi Lindstrom.

[3] "Patience," from Hogueras/Bonfires, scheduled for publication by the Bilingual Review Press, Spring 1989. Translated by Naomi Lindstrom.

[4] Latin American Literary Review Press, Pittsburgh, 1988, translated by Naomi Lindstrom.

[5] White Pine Press, Fredonia, N.Y., Fall 1988, translated by Cola Franzen.

[6] Williams and Wallace, Toronto; Red Sea Press, New Jersey; and Zed Press, England, 1987; reprinted 1988, translated by Cola Franzen.

"Bregando"
Luis Rafael Sanchez

[1] Translator's note: Rather than use English equivalents of the word *bregar*, an impossible task, I've kept it in Spanish since the author defines it throughout the text. *Bregar* is the infinitive, but I've also used it as if it were the present, in order to avoid conjugating it. *Bregando* is the gerund and *bregaron* is the past tense (perfect).

[2] Papo Swing is a popular TV personality in Puerto Rico.

[3] *Asopao* is a Puerto Rican dish which consists of chicken (or shrimp or fish) in a kind of soup, with rice.

[4] *Friquitín* are popular food stands specializing in fried foods.

[5] *Alcapurria* is a tasty *fritura* (fried dish) made with banana and yautia (a tuber) and filled with red meat or crab meat.

[6] *Pionono* is another kind of *fritura* with the outside made of ripe plantain and filled with ground beef.

[7] *Jíbaro envuelto* is a *fritura* made of ripe plantain and wheat flour.

Being America

§*Yanicleca* is a *fritura* made with wheat flour, baking soda, milk, salt and sugar.

[9]*Almojábana* is a *fritura* made with milk, rice flour and melted cheese on the inside.

[10]*Nicolás y los demás* is a film made by the well-known Puerto Rican actor, screenwriter, poet and filmmaker Jacobo Morales. It captures perfectly the daily *bregar* of Puerto Rican experience.

[11]*Mofongo* is a Puerto Rican dish made of mashed plantains.

[12]Sánchez is referring to the Royal Academy of the Spanish Language, which publishes the most "authoritative" dictionary in Spanish. The author has made an untranslatable pun since in Spanish the words for "royal" and "real" are the same: *real*. By using *irreal* (unreal), Sánchez wants to convey the unreality and absurdity of the more academic attempts to constrain the Spanish language.

[13]Jibarista derives from jíbaro, which is how people from the countryside are referred to in Puerto Rico. Abelardo Díaz Alfaro, born in 1919, is a journalist and short story writer who concentrates on themes of rural life in Puerto Rico.

[14]*Decima* is a poem and song form popular in Puerto Rico, with stanzas of ten octosyllabic lines which rhyme. The great composers of *decimas* make up the lyrics as they go along.

"Does Art From Latin America Need a Passport?"
Luis Felipe Noe

[1]Mexican historian and essayist who has written many important works, the best known being *La invención de América* (1958), published in English as *The Invention of America* by Greenwood Press in Connecticut (1972).

[2]Mexican philosopher who has written extensively on philosophy, culture and identity in Latin America.

[3]Argentinian painter and critic (b. 1923), founder of the "Informalista" tendency in 1959. Kemble became a part of the "Arte Destructivo" move-

ment in the 1960s, a point at which his work closely resembled that of Franz Kline.

"Transcript of Remarks by Cristina Pacheco"

[1] Partido Revolucionario Institucionale, the ruling party since 1929, and the object of a strong popular challenge led by Cuauhtémoc Cárdenas starting in 1988.

"Signs of Everyday Life"
Francisco Mendez-Diez

[1] Section headings are written in a Yoruba language. The Yoruba are people of southwestern Nigeria, whose magical and religious practices are the basis of the orisha tradition in Latin America of which Santería, Candomblé (Brazil) and Trinidad's Shangó cult are a part.

[2] A priest of *Santería,* an Afro-Cuban religion which combines elements of Catholicism (such as the saints) with ritual practices of African religions (polytheism, dance, etc.)

[3] Deities who can enter a relative through possession.

[4] Rain divinity among Aztec people

[5] One of the maximum *orishas* in the Yoruba pantheon. *Changó* is a warrior, one of the most feared and revered gods.

[6] A Cuban mythological figure associated with numerology and dreams. Chiffá is a figure depicted with a cat coming out of its mouth.

[7] American tree with a large trunk. Its seeds contain cotton, which is used in stuffing.

[8] Name used by slave traders, mainly for Yoruba slaves.

[9] Indian chief.

"Border Brujo"
Guillermo Gomez-Pena

[1]Work in progress.

The typeface used throughout this book is Garamond Book,
set by Bets, Ltd., Ithaca, New York

Printed on acid-free paper and bound by
Thomson-Shore, Dexter, Michigan